LAḰOṪA STAR KNOWLEDGE

Studies in Laḵoṫa Stellar Theology

Ronald Goodman

3rd edition

Edited by Alan Seeger

SGU Publishing

2017

TABLE OF CONTENTS

ACKNOWLEDGEMENTS

I gratefully make the following acknowledgements to those who have enabled me to study, understand and share the Lakóta Star Knowledge contained in this essay.

To my partners and co-workers in this project: Victor Douville, Lakóta Studies Department Chairman and member of the Rosebud Sioux Tribe; the late Stanley Red Bird, Sinte Gleśka University founding Chairman of the Board of Regents of the Rosebud Sioux Tribe; Albert White Hat Sr., Lakóta Studies Teacher and member of the Rosebud Sioux Tribe; Florentine Blue Thunder, artist, Lakóta Studies teacher and member of the Rosebud Sioux Tribe; Charlotte A. Black Elk, author, member of the Rosebud Sioux Tribe, and the Oyuḣpe Tiośpaye; Ben Black Bear, Jr., former Vice-President of the Rosebud Sioux Tribe, Executive Director of the Tribal Land Enterprise, ordained Deacon of the Roman Catholic Church, member of the Black Hills Sioux Nation Treaty Council, and an authority on the Lakóta language.

To the Lakóta people – who have for decades hidden the star knowledge in their hearts, but who are now reaching over the walls of prejudice to share it with their brothers and sisters on every continent.

And to the Spirits and Powers – who have their lives in and among the stars. They have revealed themselves and their knowledge to the People, in order that all may live in unity.

This edition is dedicated to the memory of Stanley Red Bird and of Ronald Goodman.

PREFACE

Naked Eye Astronomy

Ray A. Williamson, Senior Fellow
Space Policy Institute
George Washington University
Washington, DC 20052

Throughout the Americas, whether from the stars, the Sun, or the Moon, Native North Americans groups throughout the hemisphere have been avid watchers of the sky and have carefully noted the cyclic patterns of the Sun and Moon, the stars and planets (Aveni 1977, 1989; Williamson 1981). In earlier years, they had to heed the teachings of celestial events in order to survive.

For agricultural groups, watching the regular motions of the sky made possible more accurate timing of planting and harvesting activities. Yet hunter-gatherer or hunter-forager societies also developed highly sophisticated celestial calendars. Recently, scholars have begun to appreciate the extensive use such groups made of celestial calendars to guide food production and ritual activities (Benson and Hoskinson 1985). The practical needs of food production most certainly aided the development of much sky watching. However, as this monograph illustrates, knowledge of the celestial calendar also served religious needs as well. It gave the Lakoīa, as well as other Native American groups, greater power to participate fully in the rhythms of their environment. By careful observation, they learned important lessons about both Earth and Sky and their own place in the cosmos.

One of the primary impediments to interpreting sky-related traditions is today's general lack of observational experience. Even many professional astronomers have little experience with naked eye observations. Yet named eye observation allows one to construct a highly accurate calendar using the ordered patterns and motions of the celestial bodies. Native American groups also watched the motions of the planets, as well as other appearances, including comets, meteor showers, and lunar and solar eclipses, in order to guide their lives. Because this monograph is concerned with regular celestial events that provided sacred order to the Lakota, for these matters, I refer the reader to the discussion in my book (Williamson 1984 ch. 3). The following paragraphs summarize the primary stellar and solar features a naked eye observer would be able to follow, and relate these observations to observational practices of Native North Americans.

The Stars

The dark night sky rewards the observer with a glorious spectacle — a canopy of intricate stellar patterns. During any night, stars and planets can be seen to move from east to west through the sky, providing a convenient timing device. The Klamath Indians of California, for example, watched the changing position of Orion throughout the night to determine time in the winter (Spier 1930:218; the Cahuilla (Strong 1929:129) and Chumash (Hudson and Underhay 1978:119) set the times of nightly rituals by the position of the stars.

The positions of individual stars and their patterns, as seen in relation to the horizon, also change from night to night in such a way that the constellations appear to rise nearly four minutes earlier each night. Over a month, these small changes add up to a full two hours. For instance, at the summer solstice in late June, the Pleiades rise just before they fade in the light of dawn. Yet by the autumnal equinox they rise at midnight, and by the winter solstice, they are readily visible in the eastern sky just after dark. Thus it is that each summer night the familiar western constellation Cygnus passes overhead and we can count on seeing Scorpio's twisting pattern in the south. By contrast, the constellations of Orion and Taurus are seen most readily in the winter sky, when they appear high in the December and January skies. Cygnus and Scorpio virtually disappear from view by November.

This small daily shift of the stars comes about because the Sun's apparent circle about Earth takes nearly four minutes less than the stars' journey, giving to the Sun the appearance of a small daily eastward shift. Thus, as the Sun slips through the background of stars, stellar patterns that had been invisible in the sunlit sky become briefly visible in the early dawn before light from the rising sun overwhelms them. As the Sun works its way further eastward day by day, the newly visible stars appear to have moved higher in the sky each dawn.

The first yearly appearance of a star or star pattern, in association with sunrise, is called a heliacal rise after the Greek term for sun, *helios,* and can be highly effective in setting a yearly calendar because it marks a narrow range of days (depending on sky conditions and the visual acuity of the observer) in the yearly calendar. Some Navajo medicine men, for example, watch for the heliacal rise of certain constellations to determine the start of each month (O'Brien 1956:16-17). Some Navajos have also used the heliacal setting (the last yearly appearance of a constellation after sunset) of First Slender One (Orion) in the spring at twilight as a signal that it is time to begin planting (Brewer 1950:136). The Pawnee watched for the first appearance of the pair of stars called the "Swimming Ducks" (in Scorpio) to tell when it was time to start their fishing (Loeb 1926:228-229).

The northern circumpolar constellations remain visible throughout the year in the northern hemisphere as they revolve around the pole star. One of these, the Big Dipper, was especially important as a stellar clock, both throughout the summer and during the year. The Zuni have used the position of the Seven Ones (the Big Dipper) to indicate when they should begin to plant corn in the spring (Cushing 1896:392). The Pomo watched the position of the Big Dipper to schedule their fishing (Loeb 1926:228-229).

European tradition views the stars as 'fixed' because, over a few generations, at least, they appear to maintain their positions relative to one another. Yet careful observation through many generations eventually leads observers to see that so-called 'fixed' stars actually change positions slowly over time. For example, although the pole star, Polaris, today lies less than a degree from Earth's celestial north pole, at the beginning of the 13th century it was seven degrees distant. This extremely slow movement, which is called precession, results from the continual wobble of the Earth's axis through the celestial sphere. Over a complete period of 26,000 years, the position of the north pole traces a wide circle through the stars, making it seem to those on Earth that Polaris moves toward the pole and away again. The constellations move with Polaris, causing a slight shift in the dates of heliacal rise and set over the years. For example, some 4,000 years ago, the Egyptians watched for the rise of the brightest star, Sirius, as a signal that the summer solstice had arrived. Today, Sirius makes its first yearly appearance in late July. Astronomer John Eddy (1974) has speculated that the builders of the Horn Medicine Wheel 800 years ago may have observed the heliacal rise of the bright star Aldebaran in late June to confirm that the summer solstice was drawing near. Today, Aldebaran makes its first appearance in July.

The Milky Way, a vast collection of stars that, to the naked eye, appears like a hazy band roughly 10° wide, buts across the celestial sphere at an angle both to the celestial equator and to the ecliptic. It is best seen in the evening, late in summer, when it crosses nearly overhead in the northern hemisphere. In the southern hemisphere, where the Milky Way is brighter, and where several dark patches show up against the faint background, native groups have identified dark constellations (Urton 1981). Northern Native Americans generally consider it to be a path, often the Path of the Dead. It has little calendric significance, save to celebrate the arrival of summer.

The Sun

Unlike the stars, which over a period of years, at least, appear to follow the same circular track from night to night, the Sun follows a more complicated path. During the course of a year, it appears to move both among the stellar background, along a path astronomers call the ecliptic, and north and south along the horizon. Unlike the stars, which rise and set at the same points on the horizon, when seen from a fixed location, the Sun rises and sets at a different place each day in the spring and fall, the daily change equals a full diameter of the Sun, and the Sun moves quickly along the horizon. As the year approaches the summer of winter solstices, the Sun's daily horizon movement slows gradually. Finally, at the solstice, it comes to a halt and reverses its journey.

The magnitude of the Sun's journey along the horizon depends on the latitude. At the equator, its total motion is relatively limited, moving only 23.5° north and south of east. At a latitude of 45°, two degrees north of Rosebud, S.D., it swings through an arc that extends a total of 70° from north to south. These wide solar swings make possible a calendar that relies on observations of sunrise and sunset against the backdrop of fixed horizon features.

Evidence from archaeological sites throughout North America indicate that Native Americans have used the small change in position of sunrise and sunset for centuries to keep close track of the passage of time (Williamson 1984) especially by watching for the solstices, although other calendar dates, including the equinoxes, were probably also observed. Many groups who keep the traditional ways still watch the Sun to set ritual and agricultural calendars. The Southwest Pueblos still observe the Sun regularly to set their agricultural and ritual calendars (McClusky 1977; Zeilik 1989).

Solstice watching is not limited to agricultural peoples. Native groups throughout California who depended primarily on gathering, hunting and fishing, rather than horticulture, to survive (Hudson 1984) also carefully watched the Sun.

As Broughton (in press) notes, Observing the solstices and equinoxes is still important among the Ajuwami northern California. The Mescelaro Apache, who lived by hunting and gathering, also observe the solstices closely (Farrer 1986).

Stellar precession affects the placement of the equinoxes and the solstices among the stars. As Goodman notes in this monograph, stellar precession causes the point at which the sun crosses the equator on its yearly journey north (the First Point of Aries) to slip slowly westward among the stars. Today the First Point of Aries occurs in Pisces. Author Goodman uses this fact, and oral tradition concerning the Lakoĭa constellations, to suggest that the earliest Spring Journeys of the Lakoĭa might have occurred 2,000-3,000 years ago.

How could an observer lacking astronomical instruments have made this determination? By watching both the heliacal set of a constellation to the east of the Sun and the helical rise of the adjacent constellation to the west of it the next morning, an observer could track the Sun's position among the stars. By keeping careful mental records of these observations over the years, and comparing them to the solar calendar that was also observed, the astute observer of the celestial sphere could determine the arrival of the equinox with reasonable accuracy. Goodman's work describes how the ceremony of the Spring Journey was tied to 'following the sun' through a specific set of constellations that had earthly counterparts in the landscape. Even though precession eventually and inexorably carried different constellations into the equinoctial position, the original constellations would still be connected by sacred ritual to the calendar events to which they were originally tied.

This monograph, the result the result of years of study and discussion with tribal elders, is an important addition to our knowledge of Native American sky-related traditions. It demonstrates that knowledge of the star and sun watching practices is very much alive in some tribal contexts, despite centuries of acculturalization and attempts by the dominant society to root out such 'pagan' sacred observances. It also provides important lessons for other tribal groups who wish to retain more of their traditional practices for their descendants.[1]

---

[1] This preface is an excerpt from the first chapter of **Earth and Sky: Visions of the Cosmos in Native American Folklore,** edited by Ray A. Williamson and Claire R. Farrer, University of New Mexico Press, in press.

1 Introduction

Research into Lakota stellar theology has added new dimensions to our understanding of how the People generated the mentality for experiencing the sacred. It shows that they felt a vivid relationship between the macrocosm, the star world, and their microcosmic world on the plains. There was a constant mirroring of what is above by what is below. Indeed, the very shape of the Earth was perceived as resembling the constellations. For example, the red clay valley which encircles the Black Hills looks like (and through oral tradition is correlated with) a Lakota constellation which consists of a large circle of stars.

Recently we learned of some artifacts which clearly define this mirroring. They are a pair of tanned hides: one hide is an Earth map with buttes, rivers and ridges, etc. marked on it. The other hide is a star map. "These two maps are the same," we were told, "because what's on the Earth is in the stars, and what's in the stars is on the Earth."

The Lakota had a time-factored lifeway. The star knowledge helps us to understand this temporal special dimension more fully. We can see now that many Lakota activities were timed to mirror celestial movements.

The stars were called "the holy breath of the Great Spirit," the *woniya* of *Wakan Taŋka*.[2] Thus, when the Lakota observed the movement of the Sun through their constellations, they were receiving spiritual instruction. Their observations, when interpreted by Lakota Oral Tradition and their star and Earth maps, told them what to do, where to do it and when.

The Lakota correlated several of the constellations to specific sites in the Black Hills. For example, Black Elk Peak, formerly known as Harney Peak, was associated with the Pleiades group which is called "The seven little girls,' *wičiŋčala šakowiŋ*. Each spring when the Sun moved into that constellation, the People understood this as sacred speech directing them to go to Harney Peak. Oral tradition told them what traditions to do there.

Traditional Lakȟóta believed that ceremonies done by them on Earth were also being performed simultaneously in the Spirit World. When what is happening in the stellar world is also being done on Earth in the same way at the corresponding place at the same time, a heirophany can occur; sacred power can be drawn down; attunement to the will of Waḳaŋ Taŋḳa can be achieved.

Our study of Lakȟóta constellations and related matters has helped us to appreciate that the need which the Lakȟóta felt to move freely on the plains was primarily religious. This is implicit in Red Cloud's last speech to the People in 1903:

"We told them (government officials) that the supernatural powers, Taḳu Waḳaŋ, had given to the Lakȟóta the buffalo for food and clothing. We told them that where the buffalo ranged, that was our country. We told them that the country of the buffalo was the country of the Lakȟóta. We told them that the buffalo have their country and the Lakȟóta must have the buffalo."[3]

The repeated use of the word "must" in his speech is the sign that what Red Cloud is referring to is religious duty and not merely economic necessity or political control. He is referring to the need for religious <u>freedom</u>.

There is much he did not tell government officials. Perhaps because he already knew they would disregard the importance of such information, he did not tell them that among the animals, the buffalo is the embodiment of the power of the Sun, that in following the buffalo, the Lakȟóta were following the Sun on Earth, and that following the Sun and the buffalo was part of living in harmony and balance with the sacred powers of the universe.

Each spring, a small group composed of especially devoted members from several Lakȟóta bands journeyed through the Black Hills, synchronizing their movements to the motions of the Sun along the ecliptic. As the Sun moved into a particular Lakȟóta constellation, they traveled to the site correlated with that constellation and held ceremonies there. Finally, they arrived at *Maⁿto Tiⁿpila* (otherwise known as Devil's Tower) at midsummer for the Sun Dance where they were joined by many western Lakȟóta bands.

Thus far, our research has provided information mainly about the three months from spring equinox to summer solstice. Elder women have told us, "After Sun Dance, that time belonged to us." They were referring, of course, to the gathering of fruits and berries. This, too, was a time-factored activity. We can see that from the lunar calendar which names midsummer "The Moon When Chokecherries Are Black," and the following month as "The Moon When Plums Are Red."

The fourth chapter, "Mirroring," discusses what has become the central symbol of Lakȟóta stellar theology:

Several meanings for this symbol emerge. First, the vortex above is a star, and the vortex below is the related earth site. Second, the vortex above is the Sun, and the vortex below represents Sun Dancers. Furthermore, the vortex with its apex pointed up is also in the shape of a tiⁿpi, and in the fourth chapter the construction of a tiⁿpi is described as replicating the creation of the world.

The fifth chapter outlines the after-death journey of the spirit among the stars. This account entails discussion of the Lakȟóta teaching about the dual nature of a human being: matter and spirit. The mirroring archetype appears again because "the place of the spirits," *wanáǧi yaⁿta,* represents the ideal values of *tióšⁿpaye,* "the extended family," which the tribe attempts to embody in its everyday life.

The sixth chapter tells the story of "The Hand," the *naⁿpe* constellation and the Fallen Star stories related to it. We find a familiar Lakȟóta teaching about the necessity of sacrifice in order to renew life. Here, however, it is given in the context of the annual disappearance of certain stars before midsummer and their reappearance before winter solstice.

Chapter seven, "Lakȟóta mandala," shows how Lakȟóta women used abstract stellar symbols to convey sacred knowledge while making beautiful designs on rawhide parfleches.

Chapter eight describes how Lakȟóta midwives guided mothers through pregnancy so as to honor the incarnation of the *naǧí,* "soul." It also outlines the connection made between the baby and spiritual powers in the Lakȟóta constellations called "the Turtle" and "the Salamander."

It is already well known that most Lakȟóta activities were time-factored. There was a proper time to gather *čaŋšáša,* to sew tipȟi covers, to tell certain stories, to make the major buffalo hunt, etc. There is no Lakȟóta word for "religion." While it is true that certain Lakȟóta behaviors – rites and rituals – have (to non-Indians) a recognizably "religious" character, to the Lakȟóta themselves these are rather the intensification of daily activities, all of which must be lived in a sacred manner. The whole "Lakȟóta Way of Life," *Lakȟól Wičȟóȟ'aŋ,* is their religion.

Some of the approaches of ethnoastronomy have proved used useful to us, because cosmological systems and astronomical knowledge do not stand alone, apart from a culture. Ethnoastronomy, because it is interdisciplinary, often reveals the relationship between stellar knowledge and the art, ceremonies, attitudes toward the Earth, social organizations, etc. of a people.

Some of the material in the chapters on Lakȟóta Constellations and the annual journey through the Black Hills was presented at the **First International Ethnoastronomy Conference**, held by the Smithsonian Institution in Washington, D.C., September 1983. Chapter six appears in *Earth and Sky* by Ray A. Williamson and Claire Farrer, University of New Mexico Press.

Members of our project have been interviewing Elders for the last ten years. Our purpose in gathering this knowledge is to generate curriculum materials for Lakota students at the elementary, secondary and college levels. Our goal is to give the stars back to the People, most especially Lakota young people. Nevertheless, there is a willingness to share this knowledge with non-Indians, so that they (through learning how the Lakota experience the Earth's sacredness) will be inspired to seek out and recover their own traditional ways of knowing the Earth – not as dead matter spinning in empty space, but rather as our Mother, a living and holy being.

The stellar knowledge in the chapters which follow provides a new and larger context for understanding the time-factored Lakota lifeway. This knowledge enabled the People to mirror on Earth the activity of the Spirits in the star world.

[2] A similar notion is found in the Islamic Tradition where the stars are called *Nafs al Rahman,* "The Breath of the Merciful One (Allah). See Keith Critchlow's **Islamic Patterns,** p. 5.

[3] **Lakota Belief and Ritual**, by James R. Walker (coedited by Raymond J. Demallie and Elaine A. Jahner), University of Nebraska Press, Lincoln, Nebraska, 1980, p. 138-139.

2 LAKOTA CONSTELLATIONS

We begin the exposition about Lakoṫa constellations with a few stories from Lakoṫa sacred Oral Tradition essential to this presentation. The central figure in these stories is a personage named "Fallen Star," *wiċaḣpi hiŋḣpaya.* Contemporary Lakoṫa use contemporary terms in describing him. The Left Heron family calls him "a Messiah." Black Elk named him "Savior" and "Holy One."

The stories of the Lakoṫa Oral Tradition are sacred literature. Therefore, they must, like other scriptures, be understood on four levels of consciousness. These levels correspond, the Lakoṫa say, to our physical, emotional, intellectual, and spiritual natures, and these are related to the unfolding of the four stages of life: childhood, youth, adulthood, and old age. The first three levels of understanding can come eventually to any earnest seeker, as he or she grows and matures. But the spirits alone can give us the last and highest comprehension.[4] All four levels are true and those four truths are one truth. The medicine men say that how deeply each of us understands the stories the stories tells us about the level we have attained in our *own* lives. The following are paraphrases of several Fallen Star stories:

Long, long ago, two young Lakoṫa women were out one night looking at the stars. One young woman said, "See that big beautiful star? I wish I could marry it." The other said the same about another star. Suddenly, they were transported into the star world, and there these two stars became their husbands.

The wives become pregnant. They are told this star world is theirs, but are also warned not to dig any wild turnips.

Eventually one of them does, and as she pulls out the turnip, a hole opens in the star world. She is able to look down and see the Earth, and even her own village. She becomes homesick, and decides to return to Earth. She braids more and more turnips to make a rope and lets herself down through the hole, but the braid doesn't reach the Earth, and she falls. The crash kills her, but her baby is born. The baby is raised by a Meadowlark, and since Meadowlarks speak Lakȟóta, the baby, now named "Fallen Star," grows up speaking it too.

Fallen Star matures rapidly – in days rather than years. He is taller than normal and a light emanates from him. The meadowlark grows old and takes him to live with a Lakȟóta band where he lives for a while.

Fallen Star, the protector, the bringer of light and higher consciousness, travels from one Lakȟóta band to another, and everywhere he is recognized, expected, and revered.

At one point, the band camps near Black Elk Peak (Harney Peak) in the Black Hills. Each day a "red eagle" swoops down and steals a girl child, carries her to the mountain, and kills her. The men try to kill the red eagle, but fail. They pray for Fallen Star and after seven days (and after seven girls have been killed), he arrives. He shoots the eagle, and places the spirits of the seven girls in the sky as a constellation – the Pleiades – in Lakȟóta, *wičhíŋčala šakówiŋ,* the "seven little girls."

At another time, while a band is camped near the Black Hills, a brother and sister are pursued by some bears. A voice directs them to a certain knoll. The bears, however, surround the children and close in. Fallen Star (as a voice of power) commands the knoll to rise up and carry the children out of the bears' reach. The clawed hill later becomes known as *Matȟó Típila* (Bear Lodge). Later a bird carries the children to safety.

There are many other Fallen Star stories, but for our present purposes, these will suffice.

Figure 1 presents some of the Lakota constellations of spring.

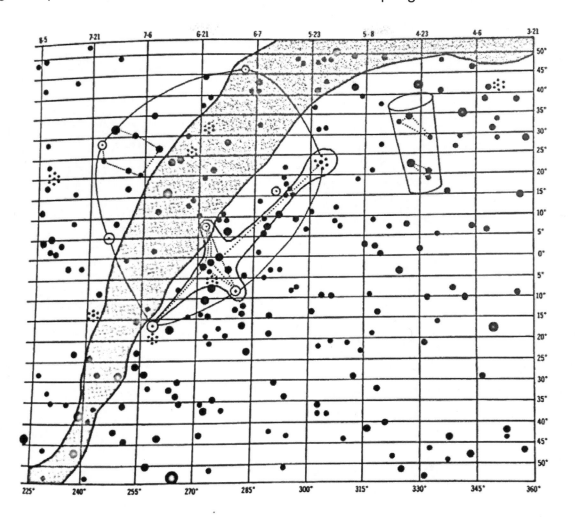

Figure 2 identifies the same constellations; as a reference point the Greek nomenclature is provided.

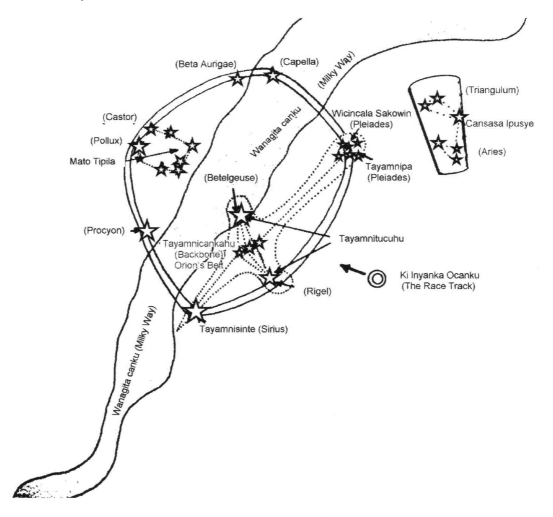

Figure 2

Some Lakȟóta constellations on the ecliptic (from west to east)

1)   *Ċaŋśaśa Iṗusye* – Dried Willow;

2)   *Wičiŋċala śaḳowiŋ* – Seven Little Girls;

3)   *Ťayamni* (the group) – An Animal;

4)   *Ki Iŋyanḳa Oċaŋḳu* – The Race Track;

5)   *Maťo Tiṗila* – The Bear's Lodge.

We know from Oral Tradition that many of the Lakoṫa bands wintered in western South Dakota and Nebraska. We know that one of the main ritual tasks of winter (to be completed before the coming of the first thunders the following spring) was the gathering of the red willow, ċaŋṡaṡa. The inner bark of this tree (red dogwood, **Cornus stolonifera**) is the principal ingredient in the smoking mixture used while praying with the Sacred Pipe.[4]

Thus Ċaŋṡaṡa Iṗusye, "Dried Willow," is the constellation that denotes the end of winter or beginning of spring. The constellation, formed with stars in Triangulum and Aries, looks like a branch with the bark stripped off. When the Sun enters it, their conjunction announces that the People are (or should be) ready to follow the teachings of the Sacred Pipe for another year.[5]

Ċaŋṡaṡa Iṗusye was also an esoteric shamanic expression for the wooden spoon used ritually to carry a live coal from the fireplace to light the contents of the Pipe during the smoking of the Sacred Pipe. With this meaning intended, the Big Dipper was sometimes called Ċaŋṡaṡa Iṗusye.

If the Big Dipper is a ritual spoon, then a celestial pipe ceremony is implied. What is the live coal? What is the Pipe?

The live coal is the Sun, and the Pipe is the zodiacal constellation Ċaŋṡaṡa Iṗusye, wherein this phrase means – as it normally does – "dried willow." This needs some clarification.

Since dried willow is the principal ingredient in the smoking mixture, then, by a figure of speech (called in Greek *synecdoche*) where the part represents or stands for the whole, the dried willow here stands for the whole Sacred Pipe. Further, as this constellation is in Triangulum and Aries, and was recognized as an end of winter/beginning of spring constellation, we can also supply the time when the celestial Pipe ceremony was performed.

On the morning of the vernal equinox, the Big Dipper was used by the Wakaŋ Wašṫe, "The sacred above powers of good," to carry the live coal of the Sun to the Pipe in the "Dried Willow" constellation in Triangulum and Aries.

What is the significance of this? Why was the celestial Pipe ceremony being performed?

It was a cosmic ritual to rekindle the sacred fire of life on Earth. The higher powers, using stars and the Sun, performed a celestial Pipe ceremony to regenerate the Earth. This cosmic ritual was mirrored by the People still in their winter camps, performing the same ceremony at the same crucial time, participating thereby in the renewal of temporality, in the regeneration of a new and living Earth.

East of "Dried Willow," the next Lakoṫa constellation is identical to the Pleiades. Its name, "Seven Little Girls," or Wiċiŋċala šaḳowiŋ, links this constellation to Harney Peak (now known as Black Elk Peak). On winter nights, the Elders had pointed to the constellation and told the Fallen Star story about Harney Peak and how Fallen Star placed the girls' spirits in the sky. In spring as the Sun entered this constellation, the peak was experienced as a shrine and ceremonies (to be discussed in the next chapter) were performed there.

As might be expected, the Black Hills has an important and even central place in Lakoṫa stellar theology. The next two constellations are related to it.

The great circle of stars is called "The Race Track," Ki Iŋyanḳa Oċaŋḳu. The Lakoṫa tell a story about a race between the two-leggeds and the four-leggeds.[6] The race track was the red clay valley which encircles the entire Black Hills. Indeed, the race track was formed during the contest, and the Black Hills (while they already existed and contained "everything that is") was lifted higher by the tumult of the racing animals.

There is another name and meaning given to this circle of stars. It is also called "The Sacred Hoop," *caŋ gleśka wakan*. In Lakȟóta theology, all of life occurs within an unending circle of time, space, matter and spirit, so the Black Hills are viewed as the microcosmic hoop out of which new life is born annually.

The other Black Hills constellation is called Tayamni, "The first born of the three relations." With separate stars designated as the head, tail, backbone and ribs, this animal, perhaps the buffalo, symbolizing all life, appears to be emerging (or being born) out of the hoop of stars.[7]

Just southeast of the place known as *Pe Śla*, "A Bare Place," at the center of the Black Hills, is a rocky outcrop named Slate Prairie on current maps. This area is called the "Tayamni" by Lakȟóta Elders, and in aerial photographs it bears a striking resemblance to the stellar image of the same name.

The Pleiades thus has several functions in Lakȟóta stellar theology. First, it is "Seven Little Girls," and related to Harney Peak. Second, it is *Tayamni pa,* "The Head of the Tayamni." It is also a part of the circle of stars.

[4] See Endnotes for the sources of the star knowledge.

[5] See Appendix F – Lakȟóta Constellations.

[6] The traditional story of the Big Race can be found in Appendix A.

[7] Appendix E for Father Beuchel's star drawings.

The Black Hills is understood by the Lakoṫa to be a consecrated enclosure. This can be seen on Mr. Amos Bad Heart Bull's map, Figure 3.

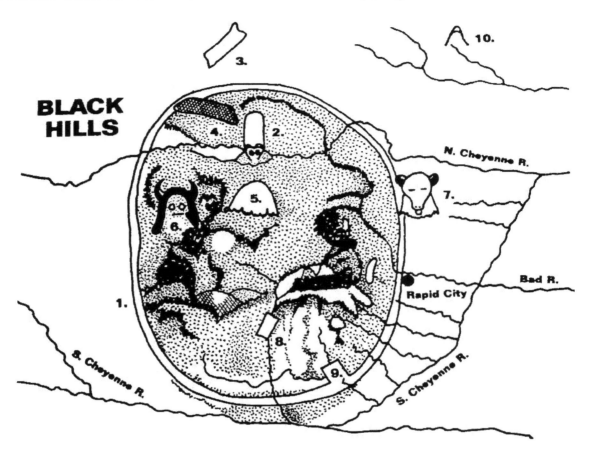

1. *Ki Iyaƞka Oċaƞku* [Race Track]
2. *Maṫo tiṗi Ṗaha* [Bear Lodge Butte]
3. *Ṗaha zizṗela* [Slim Buttes]
4. *Ṗaha saṗa* [Black Butte]
5. *Ṗe Śla* [Old Baldy]
6. *Hiƞhan k̇aġa Ṗaha* [Ghost Butte]
7. *Maṫo Ṗaha* [Bear Butte]
8. *Mnik̇aṫa* [Hot Springs]
9. *Ṗṫe ṫali yaṗa* [Buffalo Gap]
10. *Wak̇iƞyaƞ Ṗaha* [Thunder Butte]

It is with this theological meaning intended that Devil's Tower, mato tiṗi la ṗaha, was properly included by him inside the Sacred Circle (which is also the track of the Big Race), although geographically, it is sixty miles northwest of the Black Hills. It should be noted that the constellation correlated with Devil's Tower is also located <u>within</u> the circle of stars.

The last constellation we shall discuss in this chapter uses eight stars in Gemini. It is called "The Bear's Lodge," Mato Tipila. The corresponding site is Devil's Tower. In Lakota it is called "The Hill of the Bear's Lodge," mato tipi la paha. This is the hill which Fallen Star created to protect the children threatened by bears. In ancient times the Sun entered "The Bear's Lodge" at midsummer.

We may now review what has been delineated in the chapter. The constellations were the visible "scriptures" of the People at night, and the related land forms mirrored those stellar scriptures during the day. The stars were understood to be "The Holy Breath of the Great Spirit," the waniya of Wakan Tanka. The constellations expressed the basic symbols of the People, which in turn evoked their sacred stories and beliefs. Both night and day the Lakota lived between stories and symbols written in the sky and mirrored on the Earth, which through the meditation of Fallen Star taught them how to establish an authentic relation to the spirit world.

Figure 4: This satellite photograph of the Black Hills was taken from 700 miles above the Earth. (Reprint through the courtesy of the U.S. Geological Survey EROS Data Center, Sioux Falls, S3 D)

3 THE SPRING JOURNEY

The annual ceremonial journey can be succinctly stated as follows: During the three-month period from the spring equinox to the summer solstice, the Sun travels through four Lakoṫa constellations. Three of these stellar groups are connected by Oral Tradition to specific places in the Black Hills. By synchronizing their arrival at each of the three sites to the entrance of the Sun into the corresponding constellations, the People were following the Sun's path on Earth.[8]

See Figure 5:

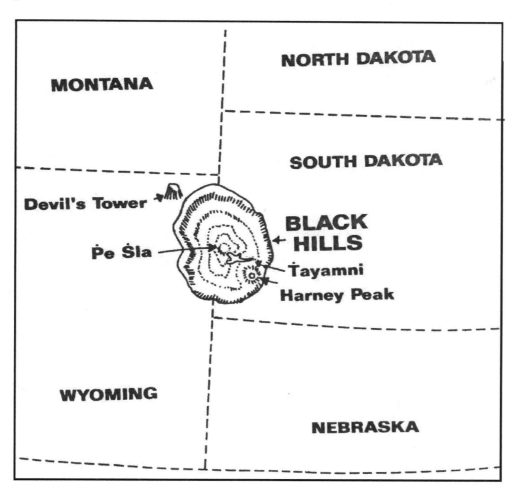

[8]Appendix D contains a detailed account of the Lakoṫa's journey.

Furthermore, being at the right places at the right times and doing the appropriate ceremonies, the People hoped to receive spiritual power from the Wakaŋ Wašŧe, the cosmic powers of good.

When the Sun is in the Lakoŧa constellation	The People will be at	Time and ceremony
Ċaŋšaša Iṗusye	Winter Camps	Spring equinox
(Dried Willow)	*(In Nebraska and western South Dakota)*	*(Pipe Ceremony)*
Wiċiŋċala šaḱowiŋ	Hiŋhaŋ Ḱaġa Ṗaha	Yaŧe Iwaḱiċiṗi
(Seven Little Girls)	*(Harney Peak)*	*(Welcoming Back the Thunders)*
Ki Iŋyaŋḱa Oċaŋḱa	Ṗe Šla	Oḱišaŧaya wowaḣwala
(The Race Track)	*(Center of Black Hills)*	*(Welcoming back all life in peace)*
or		
Ċaŋ Glešḱa Wakan *(The Sacred Hoop)*		
and Ŧayamni		
Maŧo Tiṗila	Maŧo Tiṗila Ṗaha	Summer Solstice
(The Bear's Lodge)	*(Devil's Tower)*	*(Sun Dance)*

We have calculated that the time when this spring journey first began to be performed was between 1000 and 100 B.C. It was at that early time that the celestial Pipe ceremony brought the Sun into the Ċaŋšaša Iṗusye constellation at dawn on spring equinox.[9]

Devil's Tower (maŧo tiṗi la ṗaha) is well attested as an ancient Sun Dance site. The People all knew the Sun Dance was performed around summer solstice, and we know that the Sun was in the Devil's Tower constellation (maŧo tiṗi la) at midsummer between 1000 and 100 B.C. Still, this patterned journey was an ideal, not easy to attain.

In practical terms, wherever a band had wintered, it could observe the Sun moving toward the "Dried Willow" constellation, and thus wherever that band was located on the plains, it could participate with the Wakan Wašŧe in the celestial

Pipe ceremony on the first day of spring, thereby helping in the renewal of life on Earth.

At that time, there were also prayers calling back the birds, calling back the animals and plants, and especially a hope expressed that a white buffalo would be found during the coming year.

We are, of course, discussing a period of time long before the Lakoṫa had horses. Bands or very spiritual members of those bands who were near enough to walk to Harney Peak and the Ṗe Śla went there at the times indicated by the Sun on the ecliptic.

The ceremony at the Harney Peak area was called, "They are dancing for the thunders that are theirs," Yaṫe Iwaḱiċiṗi. It was a ceremony to welcome back Waḱiŋyaŋ, a spiritual power which manifested itself through thunder and lightning. Waḱiŋyaŋ is both a life-giving and a life-destroying power that fights against evil.

At the Ṗe Śla in mid-May, the spring had actually begun and a ceremony was performed which welcomed back those life forms which had been prayed for at the equinox.[9] This ceremony was called "Peace at a bare spot," Okiślaṫaya Wowaḣwala. This welcoming ceremony included: feeding the plants by pouring water into the Earth, scattering seeds for the birds, and an offering of tongues for the meat eaters. Also at this time, people began to ready themselves for Sun Dance by fasting, silence and purifications. Bands who were, for whatever reasons, away from the Black Hills could still observe the impending time, and there were appropriate rites for attuning to the cosmic powers regardless of where a tribe or band was.

*Ṗe Śla (Bald Spot) is named "Reynolds Prairie" on many current maps.

[9] The astronomical formula for determining the "date" when the Lakoṫa first began synchronizing their ceremonies to the Sun and stars can be found in Appendix B.

Earlier, after quoting Red Cloud's words:

"…we told them that the buffalo must have their country and the Lakoṫa must have the buffalo."

We asserted that he was referring to a religious duty. We believe it will help to clarify the complex nature of this duty if we continue our account of the annual spring ceremony related to the Black Hills.

During this period of time, the names of three hills changed. Devil's Tower became Pṫe He Ġi, "Grey Buffalo Horn;" Iŋyaŋ Kaga became Pṫe He Saṗa, "Black Buffalo Horn;" and Bear Butte became Pṫe Puṫe Ya, "the Buffalo's Nose."

The triangle formed by the three mountains was called "The Buffalo's Head." During the month or so when ceremonies (preceding, during and after Sun Dance) were going on, this head became spiritually alive. After completing ceremonies at the Ṗe Śla, the People collected stones at Iŋyaŋ Kaga (a hill in the Wyoming Black Hills) and carried them to Devil's Tower to be used in the purification lodge during the time of the Sun Dance.

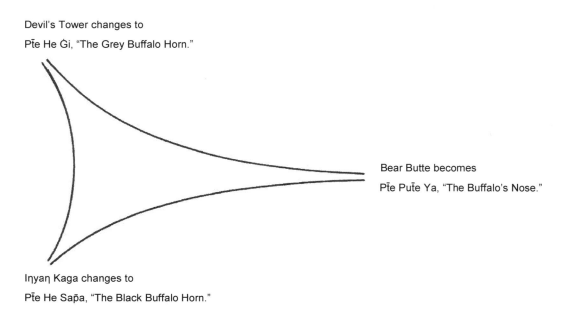

Devil's Tower changes to
Pṫe He Ġi, "The Grey Buffalo Horn."

Bear Butte becomes
Pṫe Puṫe Ya, "The Buffalo's Nose."

Iŋyaŋ Kaga changes to
Pṫe He Saṗa, "The Black Buffalo Horn."

The Sun Dance was a national event, religious, social and legal in its character. Because matters which concerned all the People were decided on at that time, all the western tribes, wherever they were in early spring, would try to converge on Devil's Tower as the Sun moved toward the constellation related to that site. After Sun Dance was performed at Devil's Tower around summer solstice, the People then traveled to Bear Butte where important national councils were held.

The Lakȟóta were made partners with the Wakan Wašte in doing the necessary work of renewing life on Earth. Fulfilling this responsibility, doing their religious duty, required that the People be able to move freely in "the country of the buffalo," in order to synchronize their movements and ceremonies with the movement of the Sun through the spring constellations.

As the Sun moved counterclockwise through the constellations on the ecliptic, the Lakȟóta moved clockwise through the Black Hills from one ceremonial site to another; each site correlated to a different constellation. In this manner, the tribe mirrored the Sun's path on the plains.[10]

When the councils at Bear Butte were concluded, the three-month ritual of incorporating the powers of the Wakan Wašte was completed also. The People were then on the Red Road. Their will, individually and collectively, was now highly attuned to Wakan Taŋka.

Perhaps now we can see why David Blue Thunder said, "The Black Hills is the home of our heart, and the heart of our home."

---

[10] See Appendix C for Lakȟóta knowledge of the Sun's position in the constellations of Spring.

4 MIRRORING: A LAKOTA ARCHETYPE

I.　　Mirroring and the Earth and Star Maps

A fundamental archetype in Lakóta thought and one which shapes first the conceptions and then the perceptions of Lakóta stellar theology is the notion of mirroring; the concept that what is below on Earth is like what is above in the star world.

In order to understand the star knowledge at least partially as the Lakóta do, it is necessary to activate the symbols and archetypes by means of which they perceive the world. By "archetype" I mean a mental pattern which is constitutive of experience.

One of the central artifacts of Lakóta star knowledge is the Earth and star maps. On the Earth map are hills and ridges, rivers and valleys. On the star map are Lakóta constellations and important individual stars. We were told by Mr. Stanley looking Horse, father of the Keeper of the original Sacred Pipe, that "They are the same, because what is on the Earth is in the stars, and what is in the stars is on the Earth." Here we see the mirroring archetype stated abstractly.

Now to give a few examples of this: We can see that the circle of stars which is correlated to the Black Hills looks like the red clay valley which actually encircles the entire Black Hills.

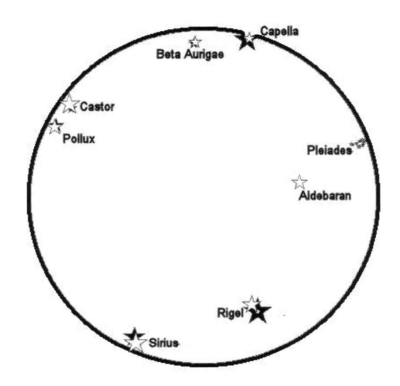

In another instance, aerial views of the rocky outcrop called Slate Prairie in the Black Hills and named "T̄ayamni" in Lak̇oṫa bear a striking resemblance to the constellation of the same name.

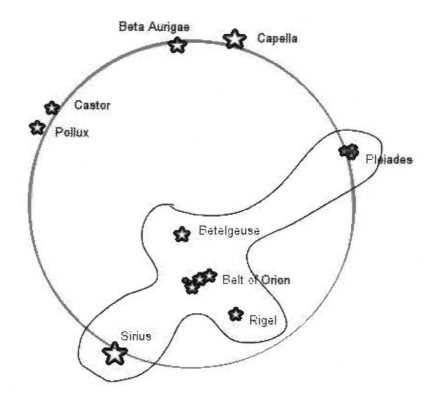

There is a Lakȯta family who own a document that combines on one hide what is usually found on separate star and Earth maps. The symbol for earth sites is △, and the symbol for the stars is ▽. These shapes are not to be understood as flat triangles, but as cones, as vortices of light. This, the inner shape of a star is an inverted tiṗi. When Earth sites and stars are combined (as they are on this hide), the image looks like this: ⴶ. In Lakȯta, this symbol is called Ḳaṗemni, which means "twisting." Thus, what is above is like what is below. What is below is like what is above.

II.   The Meaning of the Shape of the Tiṗi

Another example of the mirroring archetype is found in a teaching about the Sun Dance and the meaning of the shapes of the tiṗi. Mr. Norbert Running, a medicine man on the Rosebud Sioux Reservation, gives this account: Building a tiȟpi as Mr. Running transmitted it is nothing less than re-creating or replicating a world.

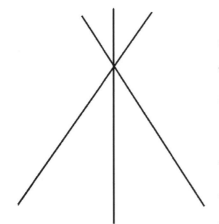

At the outset, building a tiȟpi means building a star with the first three poles. The foundation of the world is this star. The true inner shape of this world is a crystal of light, a vortex of powerful light.

Once the star is realized and we are centered, then orientation can occur; a triumph over chaos can occur. Hence, the seven directions are established with the next seven poles. The stabilization, the ordering of space, time and movement is here symbolized just as it is in the Lakoṫa Oral Tradition which tells how the directions were established by the Sons of the Wind.

That makes 10 poles. The next step is the laws of respect for all of nature. So, the 10 poles represent a cosmological morality based on respect, ohoḳiċilaṗi, "mutual respect," being implanted in everything. They are also the ethical basis of tioṡṗaye.

Finally, two poles are added outside, the "ears," which control the flow of air in the tiȟpi; air which is the vehicle of spirit. The tiȟpi and the world can now breathe spirit in and out; communicate with the higher powers.

This makes 12 poles which symbolize the 12 months, or in other words, the seasons and the life cycle.

The stellar world engenders and the Earth reflects all the stages just described.

At the Sun Dance, intentional, voluntary sacrifice is one of the ways the Lakoṫa participate in the renewal of life on Earth and in the tribe.

Dancing around the holy tree, that is, sacrificing and praying, the Sun Dancers create a vortex of power with its apex pointed up. They create a tiȟpi of praise, which also means they are re-creating the world: they are rebuilding the primal world which expresses the divine will implicit in all motion and thus, finally, the dancers draw spirit into the life they have helped to renew.

The Sun is above them,

A vortex of light…

…as they create a tip̄i of

prayer on the Sun Dance

grounds.

Thus, what is above is like what is below, or as Mr. Stanley Looking Horse said, "What's on the Earth is in the stars: and what's in the stars is on the Earth." The Sun Dancers become a star, a Sun on Earth.

Even in everyday life, living inside a tip̄i symbolizes living inside the Sun. The traditional tip̄is were made of buffalo hides. The buffalo is the embodiment of solar power in the animal world. Physically and metaphysically, when the Lakoṫa lived in tip̄is, they were living inside the skin of the Sun, of a star.

When the Lakoṫa build a tip̄i, they are building a world. When they dance the invisible tip̄i alive at the Sun Dance, they are renewing the world, and at the same time, they are rebuilding themselves. Whether star, tip̄i, world, Sun Dance or human being – the irreducible elements are the same for microcosm or macrocosm.

III. A Note on the Discovery of the Star and Earth Maps

In March 1985, Ben Rhodd, a Pottawattomie friend who works for the Archaeological Research Center at Fort Meade, stopped by to visit. He told me that Stanley Looking Horse had heard about our star study and wanted to see what we'd learned. I mailed him the latest version of our book.

Then, on April 13, Stanley Red Bird and I took students from Albert White Hat's "Lakota Medicine" class up to Green Grass. When we met with Mr. Looking Horse there, Stanley Red Bird asked him what he thought of what we'd been learning. Mr. Looking Horse replied:

"It's okay; it's all right. It's accurate and all, but it's just a small part of what they had." Stanley Red Bird asked him what he meant by that. Mr. Looking Horse said:

"When our grandfathers came onto the reservation, they had three things: two hides and them sticks. One hide was a star map, the other hide was an Earth, "Maka," map – buttes and rivers and mountains, even creeks clear out to Colorado Springs. Star map and Earth map, they were really the same, because what's in the stars is on the Earth, and what's on the Earth is in the stars. Them sticks were used for time, for telling time..."

The existence of these hide maps comes as a big surprise. Of course, we've always known about the Pawnee star map, and early in our research we wondered if the Lakota might have had such a thing. But no Elder had ever spoken of them until Mr. Looking Horse did.

Since then we have learned of two separate sets. One pair of hides with stars and earth forms painted on them was in the late Ralph Hubbard's collection. He commissioned Vincent Hunts Horse (now deceased) to make copies of them on elk hide for the Gildersleeve Museum at Wounded Knee. After the "Takeover" in 1973, the hides were gone.

It appears that this set which Hubbard obtained had belonged to Martha Bad Warrior, Mr. Looking Horse's grandmother.

We have been told of a second star map to which reference was made on p. (final page numbers to be determined).

These maps and sticks are material confirmation or "hard evidence" – if you will – of what the elders have been telling us all along; namely, that there is a significant relationship between the stars and certain land forms. Also, the connection which Mr. Looking Horse makes of the sticks with the two maps affirms that the timing of tribal movements and ceremonies with celestial motions was essential.

The Keeper among the Oglalas of this second map has said that without proper instruction it wouldn't even be recognized as a star map. Asked to explain why, he replied that this was partly because the stars as they are drawn on the robe look like a pie wedge or long triangle. He added that the shape on Earth they most resemble is the cottonwood leaf twisted into the form of a tip̄i.

I consider this reply of fundamental importance. The Keeper is saying that the Lak̇ot̄a image of a star is not a flat two-dimensional triangle, but rather a cone, a vortex of light slanted down. The inner true shape of the stars and the sun is an inverted tip̄i.

Later that same week, a friend, Chris Horvath, told me he'd been taught by Leslie Fool Bull, a leader in the Native American Church, that the tip̄i is part of an image of sacred above and sacred below. They are reflections of each other. He made this drawing.

Sacred above, Grandfather, and sacred below, Grandmother, represent the two cosmic principles which together form a unity, restoring a oneness to the One, the always and the only One – Waƙan Taŋƙa.

The Oglala star map has another important feature. Some of the Ƙaṗemni are painted blue, and some are painted red. The blue shapes refer to mountains or hills as well as stars.

In other words, this single robe is both a star map and an Earth map. The complete symbol which embodies this complex knowledge is two vortices joined at their apexes.

5 THE AFTER-DEATH JOURNEY OF THE SPIRIT AMONG THE STARS: A LAKOTA TEACHING

Introductory Notes

Other versions exist of the after-death journey of the spirit than the one we present in this chapter. Yet, interestingly, these variants have not led the Lakota into theological disputes. Perhaps this is because so many Lakota have always sought their own visions – personal guidance and knowledge – from the spirits, and also because so many people have received visions, the Lakota nation has never been given to dogmatism.

Once a vision is judged authentic by the medicine men and women, the facet of reality which it reveals is respected and added to what is already known. Nevertheless, there are some aspects of this teaching about life after death which always seem to be present. All the versions we know are founded on a belief in the reality of spirit. Also, they include traveling on the Milky Way, called by the Lakota "The Road of Spirits," and arriving at "the place of spirits." Those are the essentials.

Finally, there is nothing funereal about "the place of the spirits," Wanaǧi yata. On the contrary, it is a realm of happiness and mutual respect. Wanaǧi yata not only provides assurance of life after death, it also represents an ideal pattern of behavior.

The Lakota Way of Life, Lakol Wicoh'aŋ, summons each tribal member to mirror the good life which exists among the stars in their own Tiošpaye here on Earth.

I.   The Fallen Star Stories on Spirit and Matter

The after-death journey of the spirit, or wanaġi, is something about which we have learned while asking Lakoṫa Elders, medicine men and women to share their star knowledge.

Since the Fallen Star stories provide the theological basis for the spirit's journey, I offer a paraphrase now of two of the key narratives.

The first story has already been told in chapter two. I will just remind the reader that, in it, a Lakoṫa woman marries a star and is taken to the star world where she becomes pregnant. When she digs out a wild turnip, she makes a hole in the star world. Able to see the Earth and her own village through the hole, she becomes homesick. She braids the turnips to make a rope. The rope, however, does not reach far enough and she falls to the Earth and dies. Her baby is born and is raised by a meadowlark. As meadowlarks speak Lakoṫa, Fallen Star learns to speak it too. When the meadowlark grows old, he brings Fallen Star to a Lakoṫa village to live.

In another story, it is told that Fallen Star married the daughter of "the chief who lost his arm." They have a son. Shortly afterward, Fallen Star climbs a hill at night with a friend. He tells the friend he is going to return home. Fallen Star lays down on the hilltop and dies. His spirit is seen as a light ascending into the star world.

Fallen Star's nature combined the Earth element of his mother, and the stellar (i.e. spiritual) element of his father. At some time in the past, all Lakoṫa acquired the gift of light he brought to them.

The stories teach several very significant Lakoṫa beliefs: first, that a human person is composed of matter and spirit. And second, that the spirit separates from the body at death, returning to its original home among the stars. Thus, the after-death journey finds its theological foundation in the exemplary life of Fallen Star.

I.   The Journey Into the Spirit World

When a Lakota dies, his or her material body returns to Grandmother, sacred below. The spirit rises up into the spirit world, returning to Grandfather, sacred above. It is important to note that while the spirit travels from a material to a spiritual dimension of existence, both of these realms are called "sacred."

Formerly, there was a star in the center of the Big Dipper. Now, however, there is an opening or hole where the star was located.

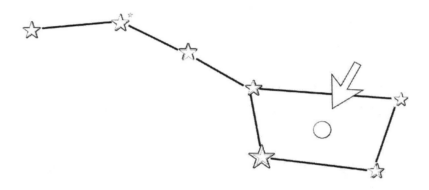

The Wanaġi comes up into the spirit world this hole which was made when Fallen Star's mother dug out the first wild turnip.

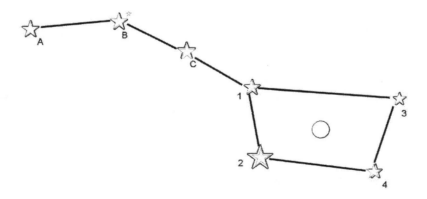

The four stars of the dipper (1, 2, 3, 4) are called in Lakota either the "carriers" or the "stretchers." Wiċakiyuhapi is literally, "man carrier."

Prayed to by Lakota midwives, To Win, "Blue Woman," is a woman who inhabits the area in the Big Dipper. To Win (or Ton Win, "Birth Woman,") is called on to aid women in labor, easing the pain of childbirth. "Blue Woman" also assists the spirits of newly deceased humans in being born back through the hole into the spirit world.

The three stars which form the handle of the Big Dipper (A, B, C) are called the "mourners." The spirit of a recently deceased person is guided by the stretchers from the Big Dipper area to a large circle of stars called Ċaŋ Gleśka Wakaŋ, "The sacred hoop." This is the same Lakota constellation which in another context is correlated to the Black Hills.

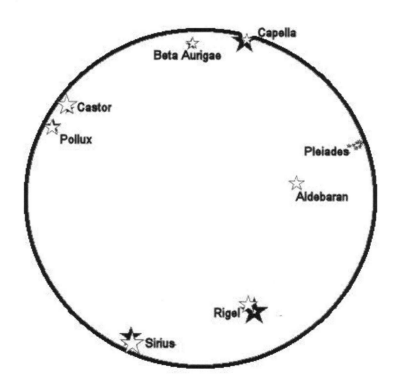

This circle of stars now becomes the base of a round dome-shaped structure or lodge used in the Inipi, a Lakota ritual of purification. The purification ceremony includes bringing rocks into the lodge which have been heated red hot in a fireplace. The opening of the lodge faces east. The five stars above Regulus in Leo are called "The Fireplace," *peṫa,* and are associated with the circle of stars when that stellar group is viewed as a purification lodge.

Then, during the singing of prayers, water is poured on the rocks, causing steam to fill the lodge. The steam is understood to be the physical vehicle for for the holy breath of Waḱan Ṫaŋḱa. It is a ceremony of spiritual regeneration, of dying and rebirth.

When the ritual is completed and the spirit is purified, it can then step onto the Milky Way. The Milky Way is called, "The Road of the Spirits," Wanaġi Ṫa Ċaŋḱu. We note that one branch of the Milky Way passes directly through the circle of stars.

II. The Place of Spirits

The journey on the Milky Way leads to "The Place of Spirits," *wanaġi yaṫa,* which is somewhere in the southwestern sky world. To the newly arrived spirit, Wanaġi yaṫa is, first of all, a place of happy reunion with deceased relatives and friends. Life continues there. A circle of tiṗis, ceremonial singing and social dancing, plenty of food and water shared with peaceful and respected relatives characterizes wanaġi yaṫa. Only the obsessions, the insults and the injuries of the earthly life are absent there.

Wanaġi yaṫa not only provides hope for (or rather knowledge of) a life after death, it provides an ideal. In traditional pre-reservation Laḱoṫa society, the People strove to mirror this ideal of the good life in their everyday family existence, in their tioṡṗaye. The whole "Laḱoṫa Way of Life," Laḱol Wiċoḣ'aŋ, attempted to realize this ideal on Earth, and thereby to make the teaching come true which says, "What is in the stars is on Earth, and what is on Earth is in the stars."

A number of people now living on the Rosebud Reservation have had visionary experiences which took their spirits to Wanaġi yaṫa. There, they saw and sometimes were greeted by deceased relatives. They observed the life being lived in that place of the spirits. But they were then instructed to return to return to their bodies and resume their lives here on Earth.

By means of these experiences, the traditional Lakȟóta views of the afterlife have been authenticated and re-affirmed over many generations. These experiences and traditions are spoken of and shared on the Reservation, and it is because of this that Lakȟóta children can still be raised with reverence for the immortality of the soul, and with an understanding of the cosmic significance for tiošpaye values.

6 ON THE NECESSITY OF SACRIFICE

In Lakota Stellar Theology

The Lakota story, "The Chief Who Lost His Arm," together with the Lakota constellation called "The Hand," communicates a sacred teaching. This teaching describes both the sacrificial origin of the world, and the necessity of sacrifice each year when life on Earth needs to be renewed.

Generosity is a cardinal Lakota virtue. In the story, the chief's selfishness, his unwillingness to make any meaningful self-sacrifice, is shown to be not only self-defeating, but also a threat to cosmic order.

The Lakota understand the stars to be "the holy breath of God," the *woniya* of Wakan Tanka. Thus, the Lakota constellations in the night sky represent sacred utterances — holy speech, whose specific meanings are transmitted through stories and ceremonies in the oral tradition. The Lakota interpret the annual disappearance from the night sky of the Hand constellation in the spring as a divine signal of the impending loss of the Earth's fertility. Therefore, the disappearance of "the Hand" (which represents the arm of the chief in this story) is also a summons to the whole Lakota nation. In the context of Lakota culture it means that a willing sacrifice of blood is necessary. The annual Sun Dance ritual, where Lakota men and women shed their blood, enables the Lakota to participate in the cosmic renewal of life; their generosity stands in contrast to that of Chief's selfishness.

Self-sacrifice is primal for the Lakota, as it is involved in the very creation of life as we know it. The spiritual intention behind the voluntary shedding of blood in the midsummer Sun Dance can be found in Lakota oral tradition. According to James Walker's version of the Lakota creation story (Walker 1983), the original creation of this world occurred when Inyan, "The Rock," gave his own blood to create the Earth and sky. Here is a portion of the Story:

Rock and Earth

Iŋyaŋ (Rock) had no beginning, for he was when there was no other. His spirit was "Waḱaŋ Taŋḱa" (The Great Mystery), and he was the first of the superior Gods. At that time, He was soft and shapeless, like a cloud, but he had all power and was everywhere.

Haŋ existed then, as well, but she is not a being; she is only the blackness of the darkness.

Iŋyaŋ longed to exercise his powers, but could not do so, for there was no other that he might use his powers upon. If there were to be another, he must create it of that which he must take from himself, and he must give it to a spirit and a portion of his blood. As much of his blood would go from him, so much of his powers would go with it, for his powers were in his blood, and his blood was blue. He decided to create another as part of himself so that he might keep control of all his powers.

To do this, he took from himself that which he spread around about himself in the shape of a great disk whose edge is where there can be no beyond. This disk he named *Maḱa* (Earth). He gave to Maḱa a spirit that is *Maḱaaḱaŋ* (Earth Goddess). She is the second of the superior Gods, but she is part of Iŋyaŋ.

The Waters, the Sky, and the Great Spirit

To create Maḱa, Iŋyaŋ took so much from himself that he opened his veins, and all his blood flowed from him so that he shrank and became hard and powerless. As his blood flowed from him, it became blue waters that are the waters upon the Earth. But the powers cannot abide in waters; and when the blood of "Iŋyaŋ" became the waters, the powers separated themselves from it and assumed another shape. This other being took the form of a great blue dome whose edge is at, but not upon, the edge of Maḱa. (Walker 1983:206-207)

The first creation was accomplished through self-sacrifice and the shedding of one's life force: blood. Contemporary Lakȯ́ta sun dancers are participating in the

38

renewal of life. Mircea Eliade writes that human actions gain their fullest meaning "by reproducing a primordial act, repeating a mythical example... Reality is a function of the imitation of the imitation of a celestial archetype" (Eliade 1952:4-5). In order to do this the Lakoṫa imitate the conduct of Iŋyaŋ, who provides a sacred archetype or pattern. As Iŋyaŋ sacrificed his blood to create the world, so the sun dancers voluntarily sacrifice their flesh and shed their blood in order symbolically to re-create the world and renew life on Earth each year.

Joseph Epes Brown has written about the necessity of sacrifice in his article on the Sun Dance:

When man in awful ceremony is actually tied to this Tree of the Center by the flesh of his body, or when women make offerings of pieces cut from their arms, sacrifice through suffering is accomplished that the world and all beings may live, that life be renewed, that man may become who he is.

The Sun Dance, thus, is not a celebration by man for man: it is an honoring of all life and the source of all life, that life may go on, that the circle be a cycle, that all the world and man may continue on the path of the cycle of giving, receiving, bearing, being reborn in suffering, growing, becoming, giving back to Earth that which has been given, and so finally to be born again. So it is told that only in sacrifice is sacredness accomplished; only in sacrifice is identity possible and found. It is only through the suffering in sacrifice that finally freedom is known and laughter in joy returns to the world (Brown 1978:12).

As so often happens in life, lessons are learned only through inappropriate behavior. The lessons of Iŋyaŋ and the Sun Dance are reinforced through the negative example of the Chief Who Lost His Arm.

Two Lakoṫa versions of the story exist. The first was told by Nicholas Black Elk to John Neihart in 1944; the second version was given in 1986 by Ollie Naṗesni, a contemporary story teller, at Siŋṫe Gleṡḱa University in Rosebud, South Dakota, where it may be examined in the archives.

Black Elk's version can be paraphrased as follows:

The Chief Who Lost His Arm

Fallen Star announces that he is planning to marry a woman in a nearby village. When he speaks to the woman, who is the daughter of a chief, she tells him that the Waḱiŋyaŋs, or "Thunder Beings," have torn away her father's arm. She will only marry the man who is able to recover it.

Fallen Star goes in search of the arm. As he travels from village to village, he meets spirits who give him special powers. He gains a sinew and a live coal, an eagle plume, a swallow feather, a wren feather, and words of power. These gifts will enable him to change his shape, and also to escape from the Waḱiŋyaŋs once he finds the chief's arm.

As he goes from village to village, he sometimes seems to be in the Black Hills area, but at the same time he also appears to be traveling through the star world. He travels through three villages of "star people," and it is said that his son will have to visit the other four.

Fallen Star reaches the Waḱiŋyaŋs and by changing into a wren and then into a man he is able to outwit the Waḱiŋyaŋs and Ikṫomi and recover the chief's arm. By using the other powers he was given, he is able to flee successfully. He restores the arm to the chief, marries the daughter and they have a son (DeMallie 1984:404-409).

Like many Lakoṫa stories, "The Chief Who Lost His Arm," initially describes how *not* to behave. The story implies that the chief is selfish, and that his selfishness threatens to interrupt the cosmic cycle. Continuation of life requires renewal through self-sacrifice. Because the Chief apparently refuses to make any offering of himself, divine intervention becomes necessary. First, "The Thunders," the Waḱiŋyaŋs, tear off his arm and hide it. Second, Fallen Star (who has a human mother, and a father who is a star, that is a spirit) must complete the process by struggling with the Thunders and regaining the arm.

The first part of the story shows us that it is the duty of the Waḱiŋyaŋs to take away the fertility of the Earth every year. They also take away each year the masculine power to fertilize the Earth which the arm symbolizes. This is an essential function of the Waḱiŋyaŋs in the annual cycle of life, death, and renewal. The power to generate life is gained, lost and regained each year, but only through sacrifice.

The cosmic cycle is presented on the narrative level as a typical hero story that even includes elements of kingly succession. The chief does not voluntarily give his arm to the Thunders. He represents the old year. That is why restoring his arm does not really restore him. Fallen Star has earned the spiritual right and the generative power that the arm symbolizes. Fallen Star represents the new chief and the new year. He has proved himself worthy of marrying the chief's daughter. The daughter is homologous with a young and fertile Mother Earth. The son born to Fallen Star and the chief's daughter stands for the emergent life forms of a renewed Earth. The fact that Fallen Star is sometimes in the sky and sometimes on Earth symbolically links the two and reinforces the importance of people's living according to precepts set forth in the sky.

What the old chief loses involuntarily, the Sun Dancers vow to recover. They overcome chaos, death, and the Earth's infertility by doing as Iŋyaŋ and Fallen Star did. Thus, as Iŋyaŋ created the world by shedding his blood, the Sun Dancers hope to re-create and renew the world by voluntarily sacrificing their blood. Symbolically, they are also recovering the chief's lost arm.

The Hand constellation (*napē*) which was identified for us by Mr. William Red Bird of the Rosebud Sioux Reservation in 1986, occurs in Orion, and represents the hand that the Chief lost when he lost his arm. The belt of Orion is the wrist. The sword of Orion is the thumb. Rigel makes the index finger. He star for the little finger is the northernmost star in Eridanus, Beta Eridani.

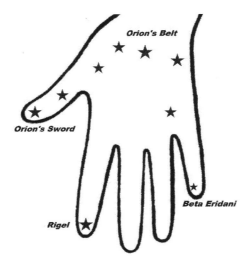

Years ago, *napē* had its heliacal setting a short time before midsummer. This was the period when summer solstice occurred in *Mato Tipila,* "The Bear's Lodge," a Lakota constellation consisting of eight stars around Gemini. As stated earlier, the Lakota regard the disappearance from the night sky of the Hand constellation as a divine signal of impending loss of fertility. This necessary annual loss is represented in the story by the Waḱiŋyaŋs who tear off the Chief's arm. It is also an announcement that sacrifice will be required to recover the power to fertilize the Earth again.

The reappearance in the night sky of the *napē* constellation occurred in autumn. It then approached the meridian shortly before winter solstice. Thus, at one time, the *napē* announced the imminent onset of the two great divisions of the year; summer and winter solstice.

The reappearance of the Hand is a cosmic affirmation that the blood sacrifice at summer solstice had been effective and successful. In the dead of winter, the Lakota know they have they have helped to make life possible in the coming year. They have re-enacted the archetypical sacrifice of Iŋyaŋ. They have recovered the

Chief's arm as Fallen Star had done, thereby helping to renew life on Earth. By following sacred precepts limned in sky and story, the Lakoṫa affirm their way of living and practicing ritual, not only as proper but also as essential for the continuance of the very universe.

Note 1: As the stars slowly precess, they change not only their positions with respect to the geographical pole, but also their time of helical rise and set.

7 LAKOTA MANDALA

I.   Introduction: Lakota concept expressed through abstract forms.

The Lakota parfleche design we will be studying in this essay is beautiful, but its beauty cannot be appreciated by aesthetic considerations alone. The design is not merely ornamental, or decorative, it is a mandala. A mandala is an abstract representation of the nature of the universe. It embodies sacred knowledge and an implicit teaching about how humans may attain the center, the truth within the universe and themselves. Mandala is a Sanskrit word and was originally used only with reference to Hindu and Buddhist art. However, in recent years it has been recognized that similar works conveying sacred knowledge by means of abstract forms have been made all over the world. Thus, the word mandala has now a more general usage. Mandalas are frequently used as an aid to private prayer, meditation, or for teaching.

In traditional sacred art, whether Buddhist, Islamic or Lakota, the idea of artistic originality means not something utterly "new" in the European sense, but rather an inspired and personal re-integration of traditional design elements. And this is what we find here. It is a truth uttered beautifully and anew. The design on this parfleche expresses a Lakota woman's personal vision of her tribe's world view.

In this Lakota woman's interpretation of the nature of reality, the central symbol is the *Kapemni.*

The Lakota-English Dictionary by Father Eugene Buechel gives "twisting" as a general meaning for Kapemni. Pemni is "twisting." Ka is a "prefix for a class of verbs whose action is performed by… the action of the wind." This is the literal, everyday meaning.

45

In order to begin to receive the theological significance of this symbol we shall start by quoting Mr. John Colhoff of Pine Ridge. His remarks about the parfleche are srudying are found in a book called **Indian Rawhide** by Mable Morrow.

"John Colhoff, a Dakota man employed at the Rapid City Indian Museum said that "an Hourglass figure (two triangles joined at their apexes, ka-pe-mni) represents a prayer. The lower part (triangle) has to do with the Earth and the upper part is in the heavens. This design represents a prayer from Earth going to heaven and being met halfway by the heavenly bodies."

These wonderfully precise but all too brief words by Mr. Colhoff will need some explaining. It is important to hold to his three-dimensional (hourglass) ideas and not its reduction to two dimensions (triangles). As we shall see, Mr. Colhoff is referring to two vortexes (two tipi shapes) joined at their apexes, and turning.

At one point in our research into Lakota Star Knowledge, we were told that a symbol for both stars and the Sun is a vortex with the apex pointing down.

Mr. Norbert Running, Medicine Man and Sun Dance leader on the Rosebud Reservation, explained that the Sun Dancers create with sacrifices and prayers an invisible tipi (or vortex) of praise as they dance around the holy tree at the center.

Sun above, Holy Tree below: ⧖ And the connection between them is prayer.

The Lakota have maps of the Earth and charts of the stars, and "they are the same," said Mr. Stanley Looking Horse, father of the Keeper of the original Sacred Pipe, "because what's on the Earth is in the stars. And what's in the stars is on the Earth. This mirroring principle will prove central to understanding the parfleche design.

Finally, Mr. Colhoff said, "This design represents prayer from Earth going to heaven and being met halfway by the heavenly Bodies."

Also during our research we were told that the stars are "The holy speech of the Great Spirit," the woniya of Waḱan Taŋḱa.

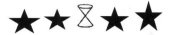

Laḱoṫa concepts about the divine can, to some extent, be described through making a sequential arrangement of several of their basic theological symbols. First, the circle represents the notion of Waḱan Taŋḱa as infinite, all encompassing, with no beginning and no end. This transcendent One can be experienced as Ṫaḱu Waḱan, "something sacred," while remaining incomprehensible to humankind. "Indescribably mysterious" is one of the best attempts to articulate in English the essentially ineffable nature of the divine Oneness of Waḱan Taŋḱa.

Ḱap̄emni expresses the notion that when the One becomes creator, it becomes creators, it becomes two: "grandfather," sacred above, Ṫuŋḱas'ila, and "grandmother," sacred below, Uŋċi – while remaining one.

The symbol shows a division into above and below, with masculine and feminine attributes. As grandfather and grandmother they are separate yet not separated. The two creators express the aspects of the One, Waḱan Taŋḱa. And it is through the power of their "sacred talk," woglaḱa wakaŋ, their prayerful and mirrored dialogue that the stars are created; the galaxies occur; and, finally, that all life on Earth comes into being.

A third symbol, the medicine wheel, embodies further manifestations of the One. The Laḱoṫa view the universe as a sphere.

Viewing the Ḳaṗemni from above, we see first the place of the intersection on vortexes:

As a result of the sacred talk between Grandfather and Grandmother, the stellar world is created, but also the unfolding of what comes to be called the four directions. The materialization of spirit shows itself through the emergence of the four elementals: water in the West, air in the North, fire in the East, and earth in the South. Certain spiritual powers are associated with the directions, as Waḳiŋyaŋ, "the thunders," in the West, and *aŋpo wiċaḣpi,* "morning star," and *Wi,* "the Sun," in the East direction.

Thus, the One becomes two – sacred above and sacred below – while remaining One; and the One becomes four while remaining One. This makes six. And finally, there is the center point which represents the fire in the tiṗi, the Black Hills, understood as "the heart of everything that is," and the heart of a person praying with the Sacred Pipe. The heart, *"Ċaŋte,"* is the seventh place.

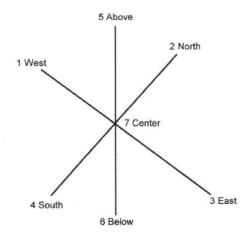

Therefore, the One becomes seven, yet remaining one.

The Lakota word for "prayer" is *waċekiya.* Waċekiya also means "talking with relatives," or to express this another way, one of the intentions of prayer is to make relatives with the spiritual powers which abide in the six directions, and also with plants and humans, stones and animals. For the Lakota to make relatives in this manner transforms a strange and otherwise dangerous world into a house of relatives, into a cosmic tiośp̣aye (extended family) where all interactions are founded on mutual respect. A Lakota can then look from the Sun to the buffalo, from the eagle to the cottonwood and say truthfully and gratefully, *miṫakuye oyaśiŋ;* "all my relatives" — "These are all my relatives."

There is, of course, more to be said, but these are the necessary explanations of Mr. Colhoff's words, such that we may now look at the parfleche design with better understanding.

II.   Interpretation of the design.

The principal model for the presentation of ideas in this design is through the mirroring of certain basic Lakota symbols. Of course, this mirroring gives an artistic balance and symmetry to the overall pattern, but it is this theological significance of the mirroring which shall mainly concern us here.

First, we see Grandmother Earth's prayer as the triangle rising out of the Earth, which is represented as a sacred mountain, as tiṗi, as vortex;

And then its mirrored image representing Grandfather, sacred above:

We see the two vortices meeting at their two apexes, and we know they are spinning. The twisting represents the "sacred talk," the movement of prayerful and creative speech going on between the grandparents, the spouses.

Next, we observe the triangles on the left and right. Together with the triangles at the peaks of the two sacred mountains, they make a four directions symbol which meets at the center.

Once the center, čokata, is established by the k̄ap̄emni, then spiritual power rays out and flows in at the six directions: West, North, East, South, above, and below.

The triangles on the mountains serve a double purpose in this mandala: they are sacred above and sacred below, but also they are North and South. If we separate that double function, the perspective becomes at once three-dimensional, with the four direction triangles representing the horizontal plane and the two mountains representing the vertical perspective.

Therefore, this: implies this:

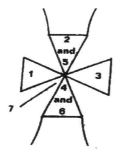   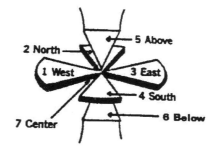

We now have seven directions: 1 West, 2 North, 3 East, 4 South, 5 above, 6 above, 7 below. The seventh direction is the place where all six apexes converge. This "center" represents fire in the tipi, the human heart, and the heart of the Earth, which to the Lakota is the Black Hills.

Moving away from the center and the directions, we come next to the large winged images which mirror each other. The bird, especially the eagle, is a Lakota symbol for that power which mediates (or carries) prayer from below to above.

The mirroring of the winged image here (each with a triangle, as it were, within it) implies that this same power is sent back down in response. In other words, prayer is answered. The Lakota live in a compassionate universe.

Finally there is the border pattern. It contains seven images, three dark and four light, on each side. Any border expresses limits. Thus, from one perspective, the dark triangles might be mountains, for example, the mountains on the horizon around the Black Hills. However, the context here is, I believe, more comprehensive. The seven represent proper orientation to the spiritual powers of the macrocosm. This is achieved through prayer. As we have seen, "prayer" in Lakota also means making relatives of the spiritual powers in the seven directions. Implied in the mirroring of borders is the notion that the Lakota are a people who, having first achieved the center, the fire, and the heart, are now accurately oriented through a prayerful life, "the Lakota way of life," Lakhol wicoh'aŋ, to the sources of power in the macrocosm as well.

III. Summation

This parfleche contains a mandala which expresses a Lakota woman's personal vision of the tribe's world view. The mandala characterizes the nature of this universe as prayer, that is, as "sacred talk" between the primal relatives: sacred below, grandmother, and sacred above, grandfather.

It is the mirroring in this work which expresses by various artistic means the concept of reciprocity.

The design affirms that, for the Lakota, the cosmos is a house of relatives. On the human level within Tiošpaye, this mirroring, this reciprocity takes the form of mutual respect between blood relatives.

The author of the mandala knew that "what is in the stars is on Earth and what is on Earth is in the stars." Her art teaches this, that the Universe is created and sustained by mutual respect and by compassion. Also, the parfleche would be useful to a Lakota woman in teaching Woope, the laws of respect within the Tiošpaye, to her children and grandchildren.

What we have learned from this single majestic example of sacred art suggests that the subject of Lakota womens' art – the variety of its expressions, but especially its profundity – is a story still largely untold. Or rather, it has been told, but not yet heard.

8 LAKOTA MIDWIVES AND THE STARS

Introduction

At the present time, there are no practicing midwives on the Rosebud Reservation. However, there are a number of Sicangu Lakota women who were midwives or are close relatives of deceased midwives, and they still carry much of the traditional knowledge about pregnancy, birth and so on. Some of this knowledge is related to the stars. In this essay, we will present a brief outline of Lakota midwifery practice from pregnancy through birth so that the relevant star knowledge will have its proper context.

Sacred Above, the star world, is understood by the Lakota to be the origin place of the naǧi, the soul. Ms. Nadine Thunder Hawk has said that at one point when she visited her grandmother, she found her at work on some baby moccasins for a newborn. A number of stars were being beaded into the pattern. Ms. Thunder Hawk asked why. Her grandmother replied, "Because those babies have just come from there, from the stars."

Vocation

For some Lakota women, becoming a midwife was a vocation. They were called to that work through dreams. That is to say, they were chosen by the spirits. Other women came to the practice of midwifery through a gradual process of being recognized within their Tiošpayes (another way of being "chosen") as one who has mastered the requisite skills and knowledge. Ms. Sarah Swift Hawk describes how, through dreams, some women came to realize they had been chosen by the spirits:

"Yes, the dream is the truth. So it might go on and the same dream is shown to her. It might happen three nights in a row. When you have a dream like that many times in a row, it has special value, and you have to go through ceremony. Then the person has to fulfill an obligation. Maybe you will be shown the same dream four times. You won't believe it. So you go on for a while and you forget it. Still it will be shown to you again. On the second time, they'll try to convince you. On the third time, it will be the truth. On the fourth time, that's the way it has to be. In such a dream, everything is the truth; that's the way it is."

Diet

During pregnancy, the midwives gave considerable advice to the expectant mother on how to maintain her health as well as that of the baby. Ms. June Left Hand's grandmother, Ms. Esther Wood Ring, told her:

"When a woman becomes pregnant, she becomes stronger. A Lakoṫa woman is strong, but pregnancy makes her stronger. The new life in her adds to her strength, so she should continue working and not be idle."

And Ms. Leola One Feather stated:

"Because pregnant women have the life-giving power, they do certain sacred tasks. At some Sun Dances, the leaders request all pregnant women to come up and prepare the offerings and tie them to the Holy Tree."

Midwives gave dietary advice. Pregnant women were told to eat lean meat, avoid fatty foods and internal organs which are difficult to digest. Some midwives gave very comprehensive dietary instructions. Ms. Charlotte Black Elk outlined this procedure:

"In a 28-day month, there will be four seven-day weeks. The first day of the month, the new moon, is a feast day. One day during each seven day week should be chosen as a day for fasting, though some liquids can be taken. During the other six days, a variety of foods should be eaten based on the Lakota view of the four meat groups: (1) underwater, (2) underground, (3) on the Earth, (4) above the Earth, i.e. birds. Vegetables and fruits should be eaten sparingly. A handful daily is sufficient. Thus a balanced diet was the first general rule."

First Kick

When the mother first became aware of the life within her, frequently when the fetus gave its first kick, this was the occasion for a welcoming ceremony. Florentine Blue Thunder was told that at the time of the baby's first kick, "The mother, father and relatives from both families begin talking to it, singing to it, teaching and welcoming it, telling it that the family is happy it is coming to them."

Labor

When labor began, the midwife was summoned. She brought plants known to be effective for women who had difficulty giving birth: plants to stop hemorrhaging; plants used when the placenta was slow in coming down; plants which were styptic and anti-germicidal, etc.

During labor, the midwife prayed to a spirit called To Wiŋ ("Blue Woman") or Ton Wiŋ ("birth woman"). This is a spirit who abides in the stars, in the area around the opening in the bowl of the Big Dipper.

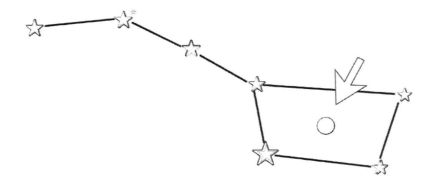

(See page x about Fallen Star's mother who pulled up the turnip in the star world and made the opening there.) Tó Wiη, "Blue Woman," aids women in labor, stretching the womb and easing the ordeal of birthing for both mother and child.

Blue Woman has a dual role. First, she helps spirits to be incarnated (or re-incarnated) in this material world. Then, after death, she aids those same spirits in their passage out of the material world back through the opening in the dipper into the spirit world, their place of origin.

Ms. Sarah Swift Hawk, a midwife, shared her personal prayer for a woman in labor:

Ate Wakaη Taηka wičiηčala waη wičočaġe Iyotiyekiya yak'u

Wanna le aηpetu ki iyeḱi či hantu.

Taηyaη iglustaηkte.

Owaṗe lehantu ki nahaη owaṗe ob'jibyela,

Taḱoja yahiηapiη kte, nahaη makoče ayali kte.

Wičozani kte.

Father, Grandfather, this young woman you have

Given the gift to bring forth life with great difficulty,

Her day has arrived. She will finish in a good manner.

In this hour and in a short period of time, grandchild, you will come out and step onto the Earth. You will be born healthy.

Cleaning

Ms. Kate Fast Dog told her grandson, Florentine Blue Thunder, that the next task after the baby's birth was very important in shaping the infant's character: "Midwives must wash their hands carefully." This was a ritual cleansing of the hands. A brew of peji hota, "sage," was prepared because it helps people to focus their minds on the negative forces within and around them, and then expel those forces.

Then the midwife or another woman, selected for her good character, who had purified her hands and herself, put her finger in the newborn's mouth to take out the mucus which might otherwise clog the lungs or plug up the throat. When she puts her finger in the baby's mouth, she may well be imparting some of the essence of her character to the baby, thus contributing to the formation of the child's character.

Re-incarnation

While cleansing the baby for the first time, the midwife and her helpers carefully examined the child for any marks, such as earlobes already pierced or Sun Dance scars on the chest. If these were found, they knew that this was an old soul reincarnating. The Tiošpaye would seek ways, perhaps through a ceremony, to interpret these marks.

Among the Lakota, twins are recognized as special. Some of them are born with marks indicating a previous life. Also, some children at age 2, 3 and 4 recollect and speak of aspects of their past lives which are verifiable, such as old camp sites. Sometimes they use words long out of common usage. It is recognized that some twins come back to restore knowledge which would otherwise remain lost to the Lakota people.

Keeping the navel cord

The midwife watches the baby's *chekpa*, the navel. When the cord dries up and falls off, she keeps it. This is said to protect the child from becoming restless and nosy. Otherwise, they say "He's always looking for his *chekpa.*" Keeping the chekpa is a way for parents to mold the child's behavior. Also, they are showing respect for the child by keeping the original connection intact.

The chekpa is placed in a *hok'si chek'pa ojuha,* a beaded pouch for the baby's navel cord, which has either a salamander or turtle shape and is kept by the family. A girl would get the turtle shape to connect her with the turtle's attributes of steadfastness, long life, being resolute and having fortitude. A boy would be given the salamander so he can gain its *sicuŋ,* "the acquired power," of adaptability and agility. The salamander can lose its tail, but with its power of regeneration it grows a new one. When the boy grows up, he will leave home, so he needs to learn how to lose something, and then be resilient and adapt. Also, the salamander is hard to kill and is a special helper to Wakiŋyaŋ, "the thunder."

Prayers were addressed to the turtle and salamander spirits. These spirits abide in the turtle and salamander constellations of the Lakota.

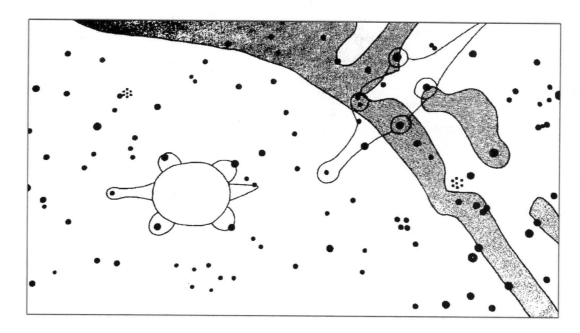

They are prayed to, in order to ask them to bestow their power or essence on the baby. In this way, the infant is connected to the star world, that is, the spirit world, and incorporates the *sicuŋ* of the turtle or salamander.

As Ms. Doreen Gardner expresses it, "The cord between mother and child is broken at birth, but the cord between the spirit world and children, that connection must be established and never broken."

In western astronomical terms, the Turtle constellation has for its shell the Great Square of Pegasus. The *Agleśka,* the Salamander constellation, is located partly in Cygnus, the Swan, and has a portion of its upper body in the Milky Way, *Wanaǧi Ta Ċaŋkū,* "The Path of the Spirits." Florentine Blue Thunder discussed this conjunction of the path of the spirits and the Turtle and Salamander constellations:

"So there's a reason why. That's why they cross the path the spirits are on. The spirits give them knowledge. Or, sometimes, a baby is identified as being an Old One, meaning that a *naǧi,* a soul, with knowledge has come back. Well, in these times that we live in, we have to have help to keep our culture alive, our Indian ways. I think like my grandmother said, in these days especially. It happens like that so the culture will be preserved."

Some Lakȟóta midwives' teachings on the nature of human beings and the Naġi

"The Soul," Naġi, chooses its parents. The Naġi chooses to be born into a particular family for its own reasons. To paraphrase Mr. Gene Thin Elk, "We are not humans on a soul journey, we are naġi, "souls," who are making a journey through the material world."

We've been told that the baby's naġi, especially during sleep, faces inward to the naġi-la, "the indwelling divine spirit."(1)

Naġi (Individual soul)

Naġi la (Divine spirit immanent in each being)

(1) Naġi la, the "little spirit," is "little" only in relation and contrast to the transcendent Wakan Taŋka, one of whose other names is *Naġi Tanka,* the "Great Spirit."

In order for a baby to live and thrive, it needs to be persuaded to stay incarnated. Ms. Edna Little Elk says, "The most important things for infants and little children are to eat good, sleep good and play good." In these ways, it is persuaded to turn and face this material world, and thus it becomes more and more attached to its own body.

Body (Niya)

Naġi (Individual soul)

Naġi la (Divine spirit immanent in each being)

If the baby is mistreated or rejected, some Elder women tell us, or if the parents are violent and disrespectful to each other, the baby's naġi may choose to withdraw from the body, turn back to fully re-unite with the naġi-la, and then the baby dies. Several Elders say that the so-called "Sudden Infant Death Syndrome," or crib death, is often the result of this choice. But also the naġi of a child may leave without the child dying. For example, in everyday life, the child's naġi needs to be "called back." A number of people have told us that when they were kids, after playing outside in the woods or whatever, their grandmas would stop them outside their cabin or tent when they returned. They would then be told to call their naġi back, and grandma would often join in the calling.

The naġi of a child is susceptible to many influences, and can easily wander off, even playfully, and thus it needs to be called back even in the most positive family situations.

However, where there is abuse, rejection, neglect, etc., the naġi may detach and not come back. That child is suffering from "soul loss." Sometimes, ceremonies are done by a medicine man to find the child's naġi and bring it back. Elders say there are many people now who are living with only bodies and minds, but their souls are gone; lost.

Summary of the Star Knowledge relating to birth

"Blue Woman" or "Birth Woman," as previously mentioned, is a spirit who dwells in the area of the bowl of the Big Dipper constellation. She aids midwives in delivering babies; she guides the baby's naġi into this world, and she eases the pains of the mother and child during labor.

Sometimes after the baby is born, its umbilical cord was placed in a pouch shaped like a turtle (keya) or salamander (agleśka). This helped to anchor the baby through attachment to both the material and the spirit worlds. Although the physical connection between mother and child is severed at birth, placing the cord in the turtle or salamander pouch was intended to bestow on children their first sicuŋ, or acquired power. This ritualized action connected them to the salamander or turtle constellation and gave them the qualities of those animals. The turtle's sicuŋ has to do with longevity and perseverance. The salamander's sicuŋ is the power of agility, recovering from injury, and going on.

Since the sicuŋ refers to intellect in general, acquiring the salamander's or the turtle's sicuŋ symbolizes activating a human's mental and moral capacities, establishing good character qualities. (1)Then there is the *niya,* "the vital breath," which commences the circulation of the blood and the breathing process and gives life to the body. So we have the traditional set of images to describe the Lakoᵗa understanding of the nature of human beings.

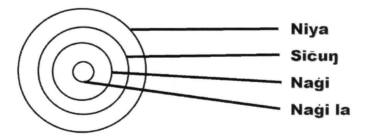

During a lecture at Siŋᵗe Gleśka University in May 1992, Mr. Arthur Amiotte discussed the concept of sicuŋ at length. He described the sicuŋ in several ways. On the humanistic level, as a power added to one's natural intellectual endowment; for example, as a talent or a cognitive skill which one desires and can eventually attain. He also explained that on another level sicuŋ can be understood as an acquired spiritual power which is a gift from the spirit world. "All things, including plants and animals, possess a special power of their own which can be bestowed on others." (See also his excellent essay "Our Other Selves" in **Parabola Vol. VII, No. 2** in which the concepts niya, siċuŋ, and naġi are explained.)

APPENDICES

ENDNOTES

BIBLIOGRAPHY

PERSONS INTERVIEWED

APPENDIX A

Children of the Four Relations Around the Heart

of Everything That Is

In ages long past, the surface of Maka was one unit. Great mountains ran east and west, and the Heart of Everything That Is stood first among the places of Maka. Many nations of the children of Maka lived upon the surface of the Earth. There came a time when most of the nations of humans grew selfish and greedy, throwing aside the rules for all the people living well altogether. Maka was distressed that her children of the four relations had become so divided and their actions wounded her deeply. She called to her children to return to her, but only a very few understood her message and came. Those she took to her heart.

Maka then shook herself; a cleansing was upon the world. Great rivers of melted rock covered entire nations, the waters of *Mni* left their places and washed Maka, removing other nations in the process, and finally some nations made the choice to no longer be the children of Maka and they were destroyed by Wakiŋyaŋ.

When the world was calm again, the surface of Maka was broken and scattered. Entire nations of the four relations disappeared; new mountains were now running north and south as a sign to the children of Maka that they had only one last chance to walk the good red road; everything had changed. Only the Heart of Everything That Is remained and it stood higher still as the first of all places.

One day, Magpie, flying in his funny little way, landed on a small bush near a gathering of the four-legged and the moving and growing things of the Earth. He heard the Buffalo (*Tataŋka*) address the assembly, "It was two-leggeds who did not live properly and brought the penalty of the cleansing upon us. I say we must destroy the two-leggeds so the rest of us, who are the other children of Maka, can live well without the destructive nature of humans." All nodded in agreement and began discussing ways to destroy the two-leggeds. Magpie quietly flew away, unnoticed.

Magpie called a council of the winged and told them what he had heard. Some said the four-legged and moving and growing things were right, and that the winged should join them. Then Owl spoke quietly: "Remember that Mato (Bear), the most esteemed of Maka's children, who is the symbol of wisdom, is also of the two-legged. I ask you, what is the quality of life without wisdom? I say the value of wisdom obligates us to take action that will allow the two-legged to live." The winged looked at each other and said, "*Nuŋwe*," for they knew Owl spoke the truth.

The four-legged, the moving and growing things, and the winged held a council and declared that a great contest of endurance would be held, the winners to have their way. If the alliance of the four-legged and the moving and growing things were victorious, they would *t'ebya* (rub out) the two-legged. If the winged claimed victory, the two-legged would gain continued life. It was decided that representatives of the two sides would circle the Heart of Everything That Is four times, beginning and ending at the special mountain of creation.

On the appointed day, all gathered at the special mountain to run a clockwise journey around the Heart of Everything That Is. Many laughed when Magpie stood at the starting line and called to him, "How can you be in this test of endurance, you who do not even fly south for the winter?" Magpie said nothing and prepared for the contest. At the signal, all rushed off. At mid-day, Magpie came upon the deer, who stood with his tongue lolling and lathered with sweat. Greeting him, Magpie hopped on. As he continued, he met others who had left him in their wake when the race first started: owl, buffalo, hawk, eagle and swallow. Magpie traveled until late into the night; the next morning he left early.

Soon everyone caught up to him and passed him, but each time he came on them again they were more exhausted and he continued on.

The race was hard and those who ran wore the covering off of their feet, leaving behind a trail of blood. As all of creation thundered around the Heart of Everything That Is two times, their running so shook the Earth that a strange swelling lifted beside and behind the special mountain. They circled around this uplifting of ground on the third and final time, but a few kept to the initial path. As they neared the finish line, the Buffalo was leading the pack, then Magpie jumped on the back of Buffalo and, within a short stretch of the line, he flew across.

The victory of Magpie allowed the two-legged to continue their existence. The children of the four relations traveled to where the strange uplifting of ground had occurred during the race. They peeled off the surface of the land and found the staff of Iŋyaŋ. This, it was decided, would be the special home of the bear. A marker for all time of the value of wisdom, and the great sacrifice given so wisdom could remain among creation.
Maka then decided that the trail of blood, shed by her children, would be kept as a reminder to the two-legged that their right to existence was one with responsibilities to everything else in creation.

APPENDIX B

Establishing a Date for the Lakoṫa Constellations

In the early stages of our star study, the "Dried Willow" constellation was understoof simply as a star group which, when the Sun entered it "long ago," signaled the end of winter, the end of the time when Ċaŋśaśa could be gathered, and the time when winter camps would begin planning to follow the buffalo.

Gradually, however, we realized that if we view the Lakoṫa constellations as an artifact, a non-material artifact, we could use them to calculate with considerable precision the time in history when the Lakoṫa people first began to synchronize their movements on the plains and their ceremonies to the motion of the Sun through the stars on the ecliptic.

So we said, if we knew the range of years when the "Dried Willow" constellation was the star group in which the Sun actually appeared at the vernal equinox, then we would know the age of the whole artifact.

This is so because the astronomer's formula reads as follows: Because of the precession of the equinoxes, the Sun moves west one degree on the ecliptic every 72 years.

Currently, the Sun on the vernal equinox rises in about the 20th degree of Pisces. Ċaŋśaśa Iṗusye, "Dried Willow," includes Triangulum and Aries. Give 30 degrees for their stellar space, plus 20 degrees into Pisces, and we have about 50 degrees. That is, the Sun has traveled about 50 degrees west on the ecliptic since it was in the "Dried Willow" constellation on the vernal equinox.

An early date would work out as follows:

72 years equals one degree

x   50 degrees

_____

3600 years ago

-   1984

_____

1616 B.C.

A very late date would be:

72 years

X   30 degrees

_____

2160

-   1984

_____

176 B.C.

Dr. John Eddy, one of the founders of Archaeoastronomy, said to me, "I don't think anyone would argue about 40 or 45 degrees."

72 years

x   40 degrees

_____

2880

_ 1984

---

896 B.C.

Therefore, to compromise, we could say that the Lakȟóta constellations are a 2,000 to 3,000 year old artifact. No doubt, the constellations had been known previously for a long time, but some time between 1,000 and 100 B.C., the Lakȟóta people began using the Sun and the constellations as a ritual artifact of attunement, aligning (or synchronizing) their ceremonies and movements on the plains to the motion of the Sun through the stars. Mr. Ray Williamson, Editor of *Archaeoastronomy In The Americas,* recently checked over our figures and confirmed the dates. Furthermore, Lakȟóta constellations are associated, as we have seen, with specific land forms here on the prairie.

We offer this evidence in support of Lakȟóta Oral Tradition which says that the People were on the plains "long, long ago."

APPENDIX C

Lakoŧa Knowledge of the Sun's Position In the
Constellations of Spring

The question here is, "How do we know that the Lakoŧa knew the Sun was in certain constellations?" Let me put this question in perspective. We know the Lakoŧa had accurate knowledge about the onset of the four seasons. However, we have very little information concerning the methods they employed to gain that knowledge. Therefore, questions about how the Lakoŧa knew certain matters, and questions about whether they knew them, need to be treated separately.

For example, we have been given an account of the spring journey. This narrative (see Appendix D) refers to the synchronization of ceremonies at specific sites in the Black Hills to solar movements through the constellations. And these constellations are said to be related to those sites. In this narrative we are told, "When the star... begins moving toward the Sun," which implies observation of the "apparent" stellar motion after sundown.

We know the method usually employed by other tribal peoples who, like the Lakoŧa, regularly studied the heavens . Also, we know the Lakoŧa had all the prerequisites for employing this method.

First. A people needs to have its own constellations. We know from the Earth and star maps and from Beuchel and the Elders that the Lakoŧa had their own constellations.

Second. Therefore, we know they knew the sequence, the order in the sky of these constellations. This is the second prerequisite.

Third. We know that there were daily pre-dawn and night observations of the Moon and stars. There were persons especially trained by the Lakȟóta as Keepers of the Moon and of the stars.

Fourth. From a modern astronomer's point of view, in order to be able to say that the Sun entered or was in these spring constellations, they would all have to be on the ecliptic; that is, the sun's path, and they all are.

Now then, the method for determining the place of the Sun among the stars is this: If A B C D E represents a sequence of constellations, and if one sees the following portion of the sequence after sundown in the west:

And then sees this portion of the sequence in the east before sunup:

Then one knows that the Sun is "in" constellation C.

During one of our interviews, a medicine man told us that the Ċaŋśaśa Ípusye constellation really referred to the Sacred Pipe. Another medicine man told us that in the early days a Pipe ceremony was done by the People at spring equinox when the Sun entered the Dried Willow constellation. Obviously, this required a way of knowing which constellation the Sun was in.

The narrative of the spring journey from which we quoted shows that the Lakȟóta employed at least the first half of the procedure just described. The after sundown observation is attested, and it alone would be sufficient to fix the Sun's position among the stars.

The cultural relevance (see Chapter 6) of the heliacal setting of "The Hand" constellation just before summer solstice (in ancient times) and its heliacal rising just before winter solstice is another important indication that the Lakota knew how to establish the Sun's position in relation to their constellations.

1. In the time-factored Lakota Life Way, to be mirroring on Earth what was happening in the spirit world (that is, in the star world) was basic and typical. It was vital in Lakota theology to be doing on Earth what the spirits were doing in the spirit world, at the same time, in the same way. The correlation between constellations and Earth sites in the Black Hills enabled the People to also be in the right place. The right place was the place which mirrored the stellar position of the Sun. The Lakhol Wicho'an, the Lakota Life Way, summoned the People to do the right action at the right time in the right place.

As we have said, during the spring quadrant, the Lakota were following, mirroring the Sun's path on Earth. The Lakota call themselves "The People of the Heart," and to them, that's what the Sun is. The Sun is the physical manifestation of the heart, which is to say, the infinite generosity of Wakan Taŋka.

Each spring the Lakota were mirroring, imitating the Sun. The Sun "wore" them, that is, benignly possessed them during their journey through the Black Hills to the Hill of the Bear's Lodge (*Mato Tipila*, known to non-Natives as "Devil's Tower"), and there, during the Sun Dance ceremony, Sun and Sun Dancers achieved an even deeper kind of relationship symbolized by this image:

In which the vortex above is the Sun and the Sun Dancers are the vortex below. The sun was in the constellation Mato Tipila, the Bear's Lodge, and the Sun Dancers were at the Hill of the Bear's Lodge. There was a meeting, a mirroring at that time in that place. Thus, what was in the stars was on the Earth, and what was on the Earth was in the stars in the same way.

APPENDIX D

Black Hills Sacred Ceremonies of Spring

All things in the universe are related, each part of creation represents the whole and the whole is present in each of the parts. Everything in creation comes from and returns to the center.

The isolated, non-glaciated mountains called the Black Hills are known to the Lakota as "The Heart of Everything That Is." We say it is the Heart of our home and the home of our Heart.

Some people look at the stars and see only distant suns scattered about the night sky. Others see patterns of warriors, animals, and sea creatures that they view as governing their everyday lives. The Lakota look at certain star patterns and say, "There is the Heart of Everything That Is, and now, I am home."

For the Lakota, the number four (4) is a significant, special and sacred number. All things important to the Lakota are four, and each lesson has four understandings. So, too, it is with the star pattern known to the Lakota as the "Black Hills Sacred Ceremony of Spring."

This star pattern is 1) an annual appointment calendar; 2) a land map; 3) a mirror-image stellar ceremony of what is, and is happening, on Earth synchronized to the other – the principle of what is on Earth is in the heavens and what is in the heavens is on Earth, in the same way; and 4) a spiritual relationship holding every Lakota to the Black Hills – the heart of our home and the home of our heart.

Wetu – when the life force flows – spring is the time of renewal and regeneration, and so as the Sun, at daybreak and sunset, is within a part of the pattern, it traces the renewal of creation and the spiritual regeneration of the Lakota.

The Appointment Calendar

The Ċaŋṡaṡa Ipusye, dried red osier dogwood, (A) would be aligned with the Sun on the vernal equinox of spring. It is our practice to take the dogwood only during the time between the winter solstice and the vernal equinox of spring, when it is dormant, and not when it is again growing.

By watching the stars, we know when the vernal equinox is approaching and collect our tobacco for ceremonies. At the vernal equinox, we begin our preparation for journeys back to the Black Hills.

When the star of the *Tataŋka Tatiopa,* Buffalo Gap, (B) begins moving toward the Sun, the spring migrations of the bison were near. From our winter camps we started movement back towards the Black Hills. *Taji,* newborn bison, calves born in the Black Hills, are considered to be special; many Lakota women planned their children so they would be born in the spring, with the bison.

As the bison entered through the Buffalo Gap, the Lakota entered at the *Maka Ċaŋ Opaya,* Valley of the Council Oak. We wre now entering back into our home in the spirit of renewal and regeneration, passing through the *Wamakaṡkan Oki Inŋyaŋke,* Running Path of the Animals, (C) the red formation circling the Black Hills.

When the Sun is aligned with the *Tayamnipa,* Principles of the Three Bodies, (D) are among the Grandfathers. The leaves of the shielding tree that whispers, the aspen, are now the size of a thumbnail. We travel to *Opaha Ta I,* Mountain at the Center Where He Comes, and welcome the thunders back for another season of renewal.

As the star patterns move forward, so do we. We then travel to an entry (E) to the *Pe Ṡla,* Limestone Plateau, and there perform the ceremonies of peace and renewal given to us among the representations of the four children of the Earth.

There are three stars in the *Ṫayamni Ċaŋkahu,* Backbone of the Three Bodies. The southern star, (F) *Keyaṗiya,* The Soft-shelled Turtle, is the lastborn of the growing and moving things — the first child of the Earth. The central star is also called the *Ṫayamniṗa* (G) and it is the firstborn of the Winged, the Four-legged, and the Two-legged. The northern star is called *Ṗe Śla,* the Bald Head, (H) and represents the head of the Two-legged, Bear and Humans, the last child of the Earth, the four relations standing together.

The main group split into smaller divisions; one continued westward (I) over the Limestone Plateau toward *Iŋyaŋ Ḱaġa* to begin preparation for the Sun Dance and the other southward over a star symbol marked trail.

When the *Ṫayamni Siŋṫe,* tail, (J) is aligned with the Sun, a journey is made to the southern Black Hills, dropping off the high Limestone Plateau through a canyon route (Hell Canyon) to where the Beautiful (Cheyenne) River travels to the four directions.

The Laḱoṫa road from the hills to Pipestone follows the Beautiful River to the Missouri (*Mniśośe*), then moving along the plains from marker to marker. Pipestone, (K) the blood of the Earth, which is far from the Black Hills, is symbolically brought home to the heart that it may beat strong.

At the alignment of the Iŋyaŋ Ḱara, Flowing Motion of the Stone, (L) the travelers are at Iŋyaŋ Ḱara, in the western Black Hills, to pick stones for inipi during the Sun Dance. We say Hor'e Win, Creation, is symbolically present at this mountain and joins with us in our cleansing of the life force for renewal and regeneration.

Maṫo Tiṗila to Ċaŋnuṗa Waḱaŋ, the Bear Lodge's Sacred Pipe (M) is aligned with the Sun on the summer solstice where the Sun Dance of the Oċeti Śaḱowin is held.

Lakȟóta people carried their central fire, which was started with the winter solstice, everywhere the camps traveled. The western bands used the left horn of the bighorn sheep and the eastern bands carved hardwood bowls in the likeness of the horn.

We call this pattern Čiŋšǩa Yapi, the Bowl of the Big Dipper, (N), that is always present and anchored to Owaŋji He, the Star That Appears to Always Be Standing Still – the North Star, symbolizing stability and constancy of purpose.

With final prayers at the Council Oak, the responsibility for regeneration and renewal are now honored and the Lakȟóta can turn their attention to food gathering and survival for another year. The sacred circle is completed and renewed.

The Land Map

Each principal star in the Black Hills Sacred Ceremonies of Spring is associated with actual land sites. The Black Hills are the mirror image of the star pattern. The sacred Hoop of the Race Track encircles the Heart, with major entry routes on the east side. The Harney group (grandfathers) are seven mountains that are among the oldest places on Earth.

The three prairies of the Limestone Plateau are shaped in the likeness of their names. Keyapiya (Gillette Prairie) looks like a soft-shelled turtle; Ṫayamnipa (Slate Prairie) is the same shape as the star pattern, and Ṗe Šla (Reynolds Prairie) looks like the skull, seen from the top, of the bear and human.

The Ṫayamni Siŋṫe follows a route from the high plateau down to a long, deep canyon entering the Race Track where the river flows in four directions, then moves on to the eastern prairie to Pipestone.

Our origin legend tells us that Iŋyaŋ was soft and supple when he created Maka from himself. Iŋyaŋ gave so much of himself that he became hard and brittle; he became *Inyan* — the stone. Inyan Kaġa mountain is a volcanic outcropping, a symbol of soft and supple stone become hard and brittle, taking us back to the time of first motion, at the very beginning of creation.

The Bear's Lodge's Sacred Pipe (commonly known as Devil's Tower) is shaped in the same manner of the star pattern, and it has seven principal valley openings into the tower. The Oċeti Ŝaḱowiŋ is a round pipe with seven openings for the pipe stems of the seven nations of the Laḱoṫa, Daḱoṫa and Naḱoṫa confederacy who came together and prayed together that all things may live well altogether.

The Ceremony

It is our rule that the pipe is so sacred that it must not be casually drawn. With the Black Hills Sacred Ceremonies of Spring, the pipe becomes symbolically present through the tobacco to fill the pipe, Pipestone quarry, the bowl of the pipe – with Devil's Tower, and fire to light the pipe.

As the pattern moves across the Sun at daybreak and sunset, creation is filling, lighting and smoking the pipe with the sacred hoop – a *hoċoḱa,* where all of creation is present, altogether.

On Earth, the Laḱoṫa participate in the same ceremony of renewal, in the same way. A fulfillment of the unity of the entire universe.

Black Elk wrote:

"Ho – and so it is that Ikċe Wiċaŝa from long ago have

Known the thoughts of Waḱan Ṫaŋḱa and his rules

They do the will of Waḱan Ṫaŋḱa on Earth

What is done in the heavens – that too

And so because Wakan Taŋka made everything

They believe these things are wakaŋ

And so what Wakan Taŋka made, we speak to in ceremony."

The ceremony, on Earth and in heaven, sends a voice that, with the four relations, we may live well in the manner suited to the way the Power of the World lives and moves to do its work, that we may all walk with our generations in a dancing manner on the good red road.

The Special Relationship

We say that Wakan Taŋka created the Heart of Everything That Is to show us that we have a special relationship with our first and real mother, the Earth, and that there are responsibilities tied to this relationship. Wakan Taŋka placed the stars in a manner so what is in the heavens is on Earth, what is on Earth is in the heavens, in the same way. When we pray in this manner, what is done in the skies is done on Earth, in the same way. Together, all of creation participates in the ceremonies every year.

A group representing the entire confederacy would make the annual journey and complete the ceremonies. It was not always possible for all members of a nomadic people, who ranged from the Rocky Mountains to the Great Lakes and from the Canadian Shield to the Republican River, to travel to the Black Hills every spring. So a certain planet's movement gathered the nations every seventh year.

Wakan Taŋka intended that we must always hold the Black Hills special to our hearts, so we are reminded every night that we have a sacred home. And all one has to do to be in The Heart of Everything That Is, is to look at a star pattern and be spiritually with the Black Hills. A constant renewal of relationship by traveling home, to that special place, with the stars.

So, tonight, walk outside and look up. See the Black Hills Sacred Ceremonies of Spring, and you will understand and know why this place is special and stands first among all places of Maka. And return, in the manner the Lakota have done for thousands of years, to the Heart of Everything That Is, to the heart of our home and the home of our heart.

Then when the Sun passes through each part of the star pattern, prepare to travel home and renew the circle, once more, that the four children of the earth may all live well, altogether – and with their generations, walk on the sacred red road in a dancing manner.

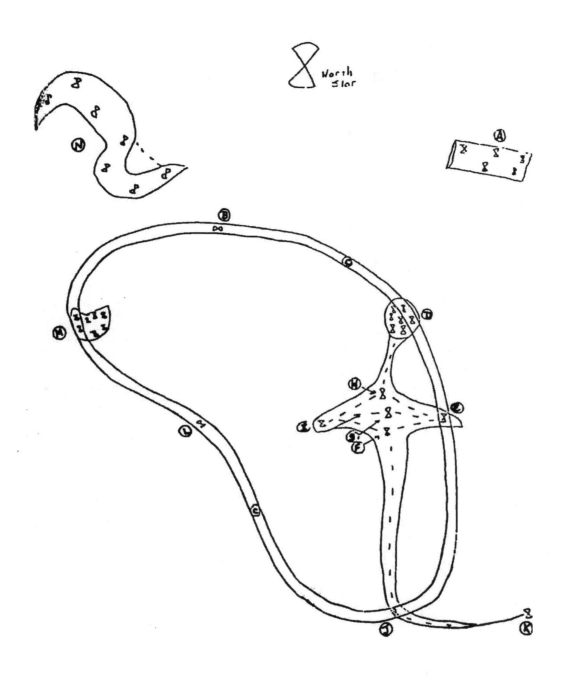

North Star

APPENDIX E

Father Buechel's Star Charts

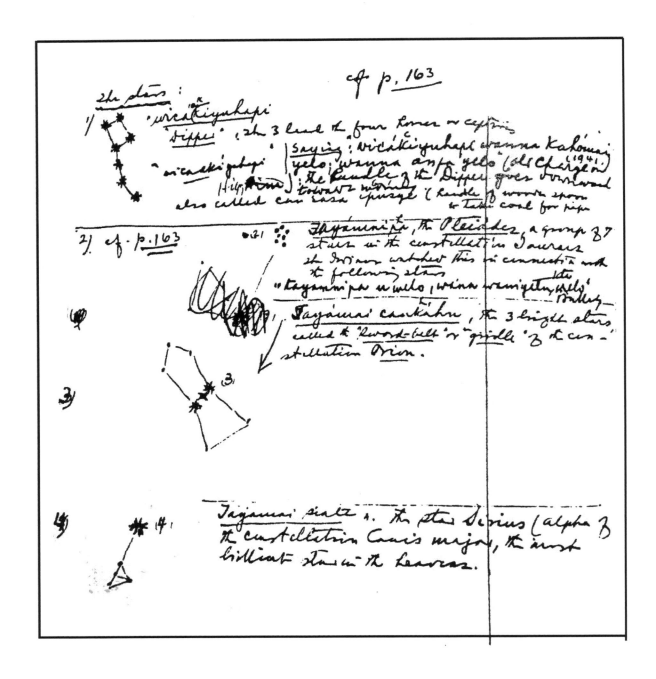

APPENDIX E

Father Buechel's Star Charts

The Laƙoṫa Constellations: Their Names and Stellar Positions

Thus far in our study, we have learned of these circumpolar constellations and nine constellations on the ecliptic. Laƙoṫa names are given first, followed by a translation, and then their stellar positions are described using the Greek star designations or Arabic star names familiar to astronomers.

I. **Eleven Laƙoṫa Constellations on the Ecliptic**

1. Ċaŋśaśa Iƥusye. "Dried Willow," consists of Triangulum and Alpha and Beta in Aries.

2. Wiċiŋċala śaƙowiŋ. "Seven Little Girls," is identical with the Pleiades in Taurus.

3. Ṫayamni. "The First Born of the Three Relations," has Pleiades as Ṫayamni pa, "the head," the three stars of Orion's belt as Ṫayamni Cankahu, "the backbone," Betelgeuse and Rigel in Orion (AKA Alpha and Beta Orionis, respectively) as Ṫayamni Tucuhu, "the ribs," and Sirius in Canis Major (AKA Alpha Canis Majoris) as Ṫayamni Sinte, "the tail."

4. Ki Iŋyanƙa Oċaŋku. "The Race Track," is a large circle of stars which includes Castor and Pollux in Gemini, Procyon in Canis Minor, Sirius, Rigel, the Pleiades, and finally, Capella and Beta Aurigae in Auriga.

5. Matotiƥila. "The Bear's Lodge," is composed of eight of the twelve stars in Gemini. They form an irregular rectangle.

6. Anpo Wicshpi. "Morning Star," is the planet Venus.

7. Itkob U. "Going Forward," is the star Arcturus, also known as Alpha Boötis, in Boötes. This star has several other names, including Anpa Wicahpi Sunkaku, "Morning Star's Younger Brother," Ihuku Kigle, "Under Went It," which refers to birds migrating north in the spring

which fly under it and Oglecekutepi, "An Arrow Game," used in this case to explain the relationship between the Morning Star and Arcturus.

8. Wanaġi Ta Canku. "The Road of the Spirits," The Milky Way.

9. Naṗe, "The Hand." See Chapter 6 for a drawing of this constellation.

10.   Zuzeca, "The Snake."

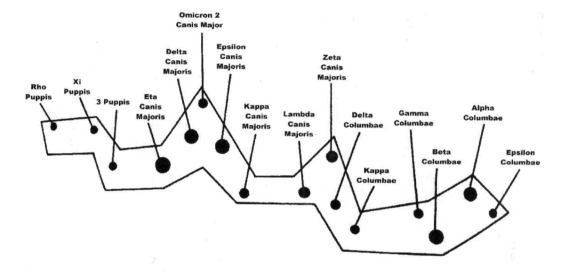

11.   Hehaka. "The Elk," includes stars in Pisces. The head is Alpha, Nu and Epsilon; the tips of the antlers are Tau and Omega.

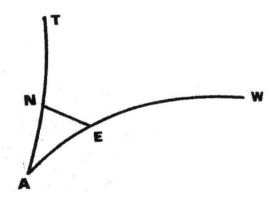

II.   Three Circumpolar Constellations

1. Wicahpi Oanilla. "Star Which Stands In One Place," which is Polaris (Alpha Ursae Minoris), the North Star.

2. Wakinyan. "Thunderbird," thirteen stars in Draco beginning with Gamma and including two stars in Ursa Minor. (See star chart on next page.)

3. **Wičakiyuhapi**, "The Dipper," is the seven stars of the Big Dipper. Its other names include "Carrier," the Seven Sacred Rites; **Očeti Šakowiŋ**, "The Seven Council Fires"; and **Čaŋšaša Iŗusye**, "Dried Willow."

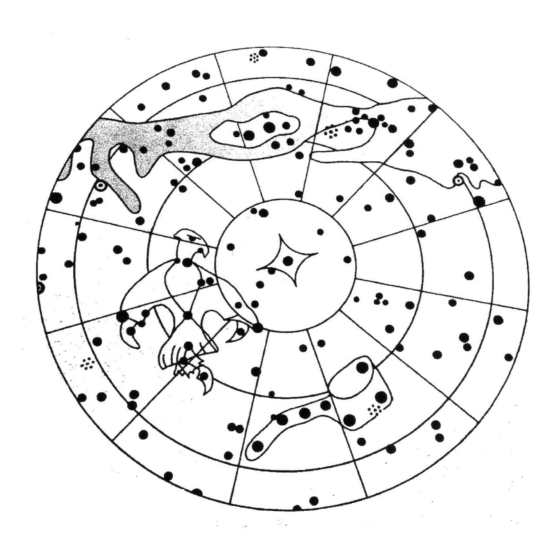

Appendix G

Big Dipper

The general term for "the Lakȟóta way of life" is Lakhol Wičoh'aŋ. Within that lifeway is a path specific for males and another path specific for females. The seven stars of th Big Dipper are associated with seven developmental stages for each sex, each stage lasting approximately seven years. The three "handle" stars chart the time of youth. The four stars of the "bowl" describe the ideal progression through adulthood to old age. Thus, the Lakȟóta have a lifeway which shows how a person can become a fully realized human being as a woman, and a corresponding pattern which shows how a person can become a fully realized human being as a man.

Ms. Charlotte Black Elk has been taught the seven stages of "The Woman's Way," *Wiŋ Oye Ya*. The seven stars of the Big Dipper and the seven stages are named as follows:

1. Oiŋ ṡa	Adorned (or red) earring
2. Waciŋ he ṡa	Adorned plume
3. Paŋ ǩe sǩa ṡa	Adorned shell
4. Isaŋ ṡa	Adorned knife
5. Ṡuya ṡa	Adorned feather
6. Nap̌e ṡa	Adorned hand
7. Wiŋyaŋ ṡa	Adorned woman

Ms. Black Elk has written, "The cosmology of the Lakȟóta was intricately interwoven into the life goals and lifeways of the People, and star patterns were both symbols and teaching tools… The Lakȟóta believed that a woman who was properly raised and taught would make certain correct and proper choices throughout her life. If she lived her life accordingly, each star of the Wíŋ oye ya would belong to her and she would be entitled to show this honor. (1)

In Ms. Black Elk's essay on the woman's way, she describes in detail the spiritual and moral maturation, and various social and artistic attainments associated with each stage.

Thus far the man's life path, Čha oye ya, is only partly known to us. More research with the Elders needs to be done. The names of the first, second and seventh male stars in the Big Dipper are known for certain. The names of the other stars are known, but not their proper order. Also, it's not clear yet what social and moral achievements were connected with each stage. Nevertheless, because this teaching is so obviously relevant to building Lakȟóta values and concepts of identity into a contemporary school curriculum, we include what we have found of the man's lifeway: (2)

1. Tȟokáhe — First leader of the people in the caves under the Black Hills
2. Hoǧaŋ lúta — Red fish
3. He iŋkpa lúta — Red tipped horn
4. He haka lúta — Red elk
5. Ziŋtkala lúta — Red bird
6. Waŋbli lúta — Red eagle
7. Wičháṡa ya ta pika — Man who everyone praises

What is remarkable here is the name assigned to the first male star and stage. In the sacred histories, Tȟokáhe was the first leader or Itȟáŋčaŋ, of the Lakȟóta people. He was the leader when they lived in the caves under the Black Hills and were hosts and servants at the feast for the spirits who visited them there among the Pté People. It was Tȟokáhe who was tricked by Iktómi into bringing the people up onto the surface of the Earth. This began the transition from the Rock Age to the Fire Age. What is implied by the use of the name Tokahe is that every man (i.e., every person) during the seven stages of life must recapitulate in his own development the whole sacred history and the evolution of consciousness of the four ages.

1. Charlotte Black Elk, **Win oye ya,** "The Women's Lifepath," ©1985
2. (a) Kevin Locke interviewed Mr. David Spotted Horse about the man's lifepath.

   (b) Ms. Leola One Feather was interviewed about the man's lifepath. Both interviews are in the SGU Archives.

END NOTES – SOURCES OF LAKOTA STAR KNOWLEDGE

Chapter Two – Lakota Constellations

Contemporary Lakota who told us Fallen Star stories include: Mr. Noah Kills In Sight; Mr. Moses Big Crow; Ms. Dorothy Crane and Ms. Ollie Napesni.

A)   Ċaŋśaśa Ipusye, "Dried Willow" is listed in Buechel's *Dictionary* and was identified by Mr. White Feather as related to the constellation known in Western astronomy as Triangulum. This was also identified by Mr. Bear Shield and others who included Aries.

B)   Among others, Mr. Harry Blue Thunder, singer of sacred songs for medicine men. Mr. Robert Stead, on the Rosebud Reservation, told us that ċaŋśaśa must be gathered only after the first frost in late autumn and before the coming of the first thunders the following spring.

C)   In Buechel's **Ethnographic Notes,** he says the Big Dipper is "also called Ċaŋśaśa Ipusye (handle of wooden spoon to take pipe)."

D)   The Oto (a Siouan speaking tribe) have a story in which personified cosmic powers renew the Earth with a sacred Pipe ceremony which is also performed by the Oto at the same time. (See Nancy Hodgson's **Sky Lore of the American Plains Indian,** pp. 73-80.

E)   Mr. Zack Bear Shield, a medicine man on the Pine Ridge Reservation, said there was a Pipe ceremony done long ago on the first day of spring, when the Sun was in the "Dried Willow" constellation. He called this "The beginning of the new year." Spirits did the Sacred Pipe ceremony in the spirit world, and the Lakota did it whenever they were camped at dawn. The spirits used the dipper as Ċaŋ Ċiŋkśka, "The Wooden Spoon," to carry the Sun into the "Dried Willow" constellation which stands for the Pipe.

The Pleiades are given several different Lakȟóta names. One of these names, Wičíŋčala šakówiŋ, "Seven Little Girls," is used by Mr. James LaPointe and also by Ms. Dawson No Horse. The story linking the Pleiades to Harney Peak exists in several versions. (See LaPointe's *Legends of the Lakȟóta,* pp. 87-94. Mr. Stanley Red Bird was told that the graves of the seven girls were somewhere at the top of Harney Peak. (See also: Gertrude Bonnon' *Indian Legends,* pp. 75-99.

A) The story of The Big Race is told by Ms. Charlotte Black Elk in Appendix A. Many other versions exist. One is in laPointe's *Legends of the Lakȟóta,* pp. 13-20.

B) Mr. Frank Fools Crow, a medicine man on the Pine Ridge Reservation, told us of the circle of stars which he said is related to the Black Hills. We had noticed that once the stars of the constellations for Ťayamni and Maťo tipila are placed on a standard star chart, the circle is clearly delineated and complete except for the two stars in Auriga.

C) Mr. Stanley Looking Horse, the father of the Keeper of the original Sacred Pipe, livs at Green Grass on the Cheyenne River Reservation. He explained how earth forms mirrored Lakȟóta constellations. This mirroring extends to all the Lakȟóta constellations related to places in the Black Hills. The shape of the Ťayamni constellation does resemble the shape of Slate Prairie as seen from the air. The shape of the constellation correlated with Devil's Tower looks very much like the outline of the top of the Tower. The seven stars of the Pleiades corresponds to the seven hills in what geologists call the Harney group.

D) The circle of stars correlated to the Race Track around the Black Hills and was also called "The Sacred Hoop" by Ms. Leola One Feather who lives at Wounded Knee on the Pine Ridge Reservation.

E) The map of the Black Hills drawn by Amos Bad Heart Bull shows and names the Race Track. See also Ms. Charlotte Black Elk's account of the "Black Hills Sacred Ceremonies of Spring," Appendix D. The linkage between the constellations and the Earth sites is also made by Ms. Christine Standing Bear Mesteth and Ms. Emma Plenty Wolf Hollow Horn.

Ṫayamni: This constellation is fully drawn and identified in Buechel's **Ethnographic Notes.**

In his **Dictionary** he writes, "A constellation of stars composed of the stars of Orion and the Pleiades of Taurus. There are seven stars in it: Ṫayamni Pa, the Pleiades of Taurus; Ṫayamni Can Kahu, the belt or studded girdle of Orion; Ṫayamni Tuċuhu, the two flanking stars, Betelgeuse and Rigel; Ṫayamni Sinte, the east of the other large stars of Orion , lying off from the tip of Orion's sword." This information came from Mr. Big Turkey and Mr. Cleve Bull Ring. In the **Ethnographic Notes** Buechel identifies Ṫayamni Siŋṫe with "The star Sirius."

The correlation of the constellation Ṫayamni with Slate Prairie was made by Ms. Emma Plenty Wolf Hollow Horn who said the land form was also called "Ṫayamni."

A) Devil's Tower: Buechel's **Dictionary** has this for Matotiṗila, "a constellation of eight stars, as they say, standing in a circle. The Gemini [twins], Castor and Pollux, are prominent among them." He was told this by Mr. Maḱalhṗaya. In his

Ethnographic Notes is a drawing of the constellation, and an interesting remark: "Matotiṗila is the name for the Devil's Tower."

B)   Mr. James LaPointe calls Devil's Tower "Matotiṗila" and tells the widespread Fallen Star story of its creation in connection with saving some children from bears.

C)   Many Lakóta told us that Devil's Tower was an ancient Sun Dance site. See LaPointe's *Legends,* pp. 68-70.

D)   Mr. Arvol Looking Horse said, "The old people told me you should go to Devil's Tower to Sun Dance at midsummer, and then come to Green Grass to pray with the Pipe."

Ms. Kate Fast Dog of Soldier Creek on the Rosebud Reservation told us that "the stars are the woniya of Waḱan Taŋḱa, the holy breath of God."

Chapter Three – The Spring Journey

A)   Ms. Charlotte Black Elk, who livs near Manderson on the Pine Ridge Reservation, has written a brief account of the spring journey which is included as Appendix D.

B)   Ms. Emma Plenty Wolf Hollow Horn, Ms. Black Elk's grandmother, has described the spring journey to her.

C)   Mr. Eli Taylor of Manitoba and Mr. Richard Redman of Saskatchewan are familiar with the journey. Both men are Santee Sioux.

A) Mr. Stanley Looking Horse and Mr. Norbert Running both call Devil's Tower Pṫe He Ġi, "The Grey Buffalo Horn."

B) The three names and places for the "Buffalo's Head" were provided by Ms. Charlotte Black Elk.

C)We have heard the entire Black Hills frequently referred to symbolically as "a buffalo," with Wind Cave as the opening of the womb, Hot Springs representing "milk," and Buffalo Gap leading into the outer world of the prairie.

Chapter Four – Mirroring

The interviews with Mr. Stanley Looking Horse and Mr. Norbert Running are in the Archives of Siŋṫe Gleśka University.

Chapter Five – The After-Death Journey

The following persons shared portions of the after-death journey. Their interviews are also in the Archives of Siŋṫe Gleśka University.

1. Ms. Susan Red Feather

2. Mr. Arvol Looking Horse

3. Ms. Leola One Feather

4., Mr. Frank Fools Crow

5. Mr. Lessert Moore

6. Mr. Pete Catches

7. Ms. Minerva Blue Horse

A)   Father Beuchel gives Wicakiyuhapi as the Lakoṫa name for the Big Dipper. This is translated as "Man Carrier" but is sometimes glossed as "Carrier" or "Stretcher." The word *yuha* can have the meaning "to have given birth to a child." Ms. Ella Deloria says "Man-being-carried is the Big Dipper; the four stars being the four carriers..." See Deloria's *Dakota Texts,* p. 122.

B)   Mr. Arvol Looking Horse told us about "The Fireplace" constellation. The five stars above Regulus in Leo are called The Fireplace. This constellation is related to the circle of stars, the Race Track, when that stellar group is viewed as a purification lodge (Inipi).

Chapter Seven – Lakota Mandala

Mable Morrow, *Indian Rawhide,* University of Oklahoma Press, 1982. The parfleche illustrated in the text is on p. 147 of Morrow's book.

Chapter Eight – Lakota Midwives and the Stars

Interviews with persons quoted in this essay are housed in the SGU Archives.

They are:

1.   Nadine Thunder Hawk
2.   Sarah Swift Hawk
3.   June Left Hand
4.   Leola One Feather
5.   Charlotte Black Elk
6.   Florentine Blue Thunder
7.   Doren Gardner
8.   Edna Little Elk
9.   Earl and Edna Swift Hawk

Knowledge about Blue Woman or Birth Woman was shared by Leola One Feather, Sandra Black Bear White, and Charlotte Black Elk.

Mr. Thin Elk's remarks were quoted to me by Charlie Garriott.

A number of people shared knowledge about "calling back the naǧi." They included Elizabeth Little Elk and June Left Hand.

BIBLIOGRAPHICAL NOTES

Interviews with the Elders conducted by the Lakoṫa Star Project are housed in the Archives of Siŋṫe Gleṡka University, Rosebud Reservation, Rosebud, South Dakota.

A copy of Father Eugene Beuchel's (unpublished) *Ethnographic Notes* is located in the Beuchel Memorial Lakoṫa Museum, Rosebud Sioux Reservation, St. Francis, South Dakota.

Most collections from Lakoṫa Oral Tradition include Fallen Star stories. Among these are:

A. Neihardt, John G., ***When The Tree Flowered.*** University of Nebraska Press. Lincoln, Nebraska, 1971.

B. DeMaillie, Raymond J., ***The Sixth Grandfather.*** University of Nebraska Press. Lincoln, Nebraska, 1984.

C. Beckwith, M.C., "Mythology of the Oglala Lakoṫa," ***The Journal of American Folklore,*** Vol. 43: Oct-Dec 1930; p. 170.

D. LaPointe, James, ***Legends of the Lakoṫa.*** Indian Historian Press, San Francisco, California, 1976.

Our taped interviews include a number of Fallen Star stories.

A. Bad Heart Bull, Amos; ***A Pictographic History of the Oglala Sioux.*** Drawing by Amos Bad Heart Bull; text by Helen Blish. University of Nebraska

Press. Lincoln, Nebraska. (We gratefully acknowledge permission from the University of Nebraska Press to reprint Mr. Bad Heart Bull's map of the Black Hills on page __(to be added)__.

B. Buechel, Rev. Eugene; *A Dictionary of the Teton Dakota Sioux Language.* University of South Dakota, Vermilion, South Dakota, 1970.

C. Critchlow, Keith; *Islamic Patterns.* Thames and Hudson, London, England, 1976; p. 5.

D. Walker, James; edited by Elaine Jahner; *Lakota Myth.* University of Nebraska Press, Lincoln, Nebraska, 1983; pp. 206-207.

E. Eliade, Mircea; *The Myth of the Eternal Return.* Bollingen Press, Princeton, New Jersey, p.5

F. Brown, Joseph Epes; "Sun Dance," *Parabola,* Vol. VIII, 4; pp. 12, 15.

G. Bonnin, Gertrude (Zitkala Ṡa); *Old Indian Legends.* Boston, Ginn and Company, 1901.

H. Deloria, Ella; *Dakota Texts.* University of South Dakota, Vermilion, South Dakota, 1978.

I. Hodgson, Nancy J.; *Sky Lore of the American Plains Indian;* (unpublished Master's thesis). University of South Dakota, Vermilion, South Dakota, 1979.

J. Walker, James R.; *Lakota Belief and Ritual.* edited by Raymond J. DeMallie and Elaine A. Jahner; University of Nebraska Press, Lincoln, Nebraska, 1980.

Note: Our deep thanks to the following persons who shared various portions of the teachings contained in these chapters:

1. Susan Red Feather
2. Noah Kills In Sight
3. Moses Big Crow
4. Pete Catches
5. Lessert Moore
6. Frank Fools Crow
7. Kate Fast Dog
8. Leola One Feather
9. Zack Bear Shield
10. Arvol Looking Horse
11. Stanley Looking Horse
12. Dorothy Crane
13. Gilbert Yellow Hawk
14. Henry Crow Dog
15. Leonard Crow Dog
16. Joe Eagle Elk
17. Norbert Running
18. Ruben Fire Thunder
19. William Red Bird
20. Emma Plenty Wolf Hollow Horn
21. Ben Marrow Bone
22. Mike Her many Horses
23. Robert Stead
24. Harry Blue Thunder
25. Ken Oliver
26. Sam Moves Camp
27. Patsy Bjorling
28. Edna Leighton-Little Elk
29. Minerva Blue Horse
30. Ollie Naṗesni
31. Laura Black Tommahawk
32. Chauncey Yellow Horse
33. Joe Chases the Horse
34. Earl Bordeaux, Sr.
35. Leslie Fool Bull
36. Ben Rhodd
37. Doris Leader Charge
38. Fred Leader Charge
39. Lloyd One Star
40. Arthur Amiotte
41. George Godfrey
42. Sam Wounded Head
43. Ben Black Bear, Sr.
44. Vine Deloria, Sr.
45. Pete Swift Bird
46. Kevin Locke
47. David Spotted Horse
48. Mercy Poorman
49. Lorraine Walking Bull
50. Glen Welschons
51. Chris Horvath
52. Nadine Thunder Hawk
53. Sarah Swift Hawk
54. June Left Hand
55. Elizabeth Little Elk
56. Earl Swift Hawk
57. Edna Swift Hawk
58. Leland Little Dog
59. Stanley Red Bird, Jr.
60. Doreen Gardner
61. Duane Hollow Horn Bear

Thanks are also due (and gratefully given) to:

1. Vine Deloria, Jr.
2. Von Del Chamberlain
3. Ray Williamson
4. Bob Alex
5. Harold Moore
6. Lionel Bordeaux
7. Cheryl Crazy Bull
8. Jack Herman
9. Robert L. Hall
10. Kathy Frederick
11. Charlie Garriott
12. Bill Emery

Their encouragement of this research has been a genuine source of strength over the years.

REFERENCES CITED

Avent, Anthony

1977 Native American Archaeoastronomy, Auatin: University of Texas Press, Benson, Arlene and Hoskinson, Tom.

1985 Earth and Sky: Papers from the Northridge Conference on Archaeoastronomy, editors. Thousand Oaks, California, Slo'w Press.

Brewer, Sallie P.

1950 Notes on Navaho Astronomy in For the Dean: Essays in Anthropology in Honor of Byron Cummings. Tucson: University of Arizona Press: 133-136.

Broughton, Jack

in press, in Williamson, Ray A., and Farrer, Claire R., editors, Earth and Sky: Visions of the Cosmos in Native American Folklore. Albuquerque, University of New Mexico Press.

Chamberlain, Von Del

1982 When Stars Came Down To Earth. Los Altos, California, Ballena Press.

Cushing, Frank H.

1896 Outlines of Zuni Creation Myths. Bureau of American Ethnology Annual Reports 13:321-447.

Eddy, John A.

1974 Astronomical Alignment of the Big Horn Medicine Wheel. Science 4: 1035-1043

Farrer, Claire R.

1984 Mescalero Apache Terminology for Venus. Archaeoastronomy 9:59-61

Hudson, Travis

1984 California's First Astronomers. Archaeoastronomy and the Roots of Science. Edited by Dr. E. C. Krupp. Washington, D.C.; Amerian Association for the Advancement of Science, pp. 11-81.

Hudson, Travis, and Underhay, Ernest

1978 Crystals In The Sky: An Intellectual Odyssey Involving Chumash Astronomy, Cosmology, and Rock Art. Socorro, NM: Ballena Press.

Loeb, Edwin

1926 Pomo Folkways. University of California Publications in American Archaeology and Ethnology 19(2): 149-404.

McCluskey, Stephen C.

1977 The Astronomy of the Hopi Indians. Journal of the History of Astronomy, 8:174-95.

O'Bryan, Aileen

1956 The Dine: Origin Myths of the Navaho. Smithsonian Institution Museum of American Ethnology Bulletin 163.

Spier, Leslie

1930 Klamath Ethnography: University of California Publications in American Archaeology and Ethnology 30.

Strong, William Duncan

1929 Aboriginal Society in Southern California. University of California Publications in American Archaeology 26.

Urton, Gary

1981 At The Crossroads of the Earth and Sky. Austin, University of Texas Press.

Williamson, Ray.

1981 Archaeoastronomy in the Americas. Los Altos, California: Ballena Press.

1984. Living the Sky: The Cosmos of the American Indian. Boston: Houghton Mifflin.

Zeilik, Michael

1989 Keeping the Sacred and Planting Calendar: Archaeoastronomy in the Pueblo Southwest. In World Archaeoastronomy, ed. A.F. Aveni, Cambridge: Cambridge University Press.

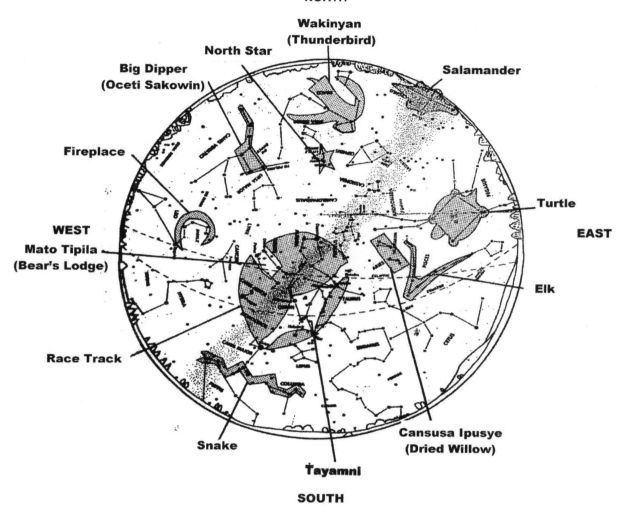

NORTH

Wakinyan
(Thunderbird)

Salamander

Big Dipper
(Oceti Sakowin)

North Star

Fireplace

Turtle

WEST

EAST

Mato Tipila
(Bear's Lodge)

Elk

Race Track

Cansusa Ipusye
(Dried Willow)

Snake

Ťayamni

SOUTH

NOTES

Made in the USA
Columbia, SC
04 February 2021